Instructor's Manual/
Test Bank

to accompany

Fundamentals
of
Cognitive Psychology

Sixth Edition

R. Reed Hunt
University of North Carolina

Henry C. Ellis
University of New Mexico

Prepared by
Donna Frick-Horbury
Appalachian State University

McGraw-Hill
College

Boston   Burr Ridge, IL   Dubuque, IA   Madison, WI   New York   San Francisco   St. Louis
Bangkok   Bogotá   Caracas   Lisbon   London   Madrid
Mexico City   Milan   New Delhi   Seoul   Singapore   Sydney   Taipei   Toronto

McGraw-Hill College

A Division of The McGraw·Hill Companies

Instructor's Manual/Test Bank to accompany
FUNDAMENTALS OF COGNITIVE PSYCHOLOGY, SIXTH EDITION

1 2 3 4 5 6 7 8 9 0 BKM/BKM 9 0 9 8

ISBN 0-697-25338-4

www.mhhe.com

TABLE OF CONTENTS

CHAPTER 7   THE STRUCTURE AND FUNCTION OF KNOWLEDGE

CHAPTER 8   COMPREHENSION AND KNOWLEDGE   115

INTRODUCTION

This manual is intended to be a guide for the sixth edition *of Fundamentals of Cognitive Psychology*. There are 12 sections, one for each chapter, and each section has 4 parts. This includes key words, demonstrations or student activities, test items, and additional resources, which includes additional readings, as well as videotapes and films. The test items for each chapter include 35 multiple-choice test items, 15 true-false, and 3 to 5 essay questions.

The test items in this manual are designed to sample the range of content covered by each chapter. While a number of the items cover strictly factual material, others require conceptual application. The test items will be most useful in examining student's knowledge of material found in the text; however, the material may need to be modified one way or another for you to apply them to your lecture or demonstrations.

A great number of these test items have been tested for difficulty and reliability in classroom testing. Generally, no test items are included which had less than a 25% correct performance rate in the class. However, given the variability within university populations and difference in teaching methods, it is recommended that a performance rate be scored for each item within your own class. If there is less than 10 to 15% of the students scoring an item wrong, then it is assumed that there is ambiguity within the test sample, and that item should be dealt with accordingly. In addition, it is recommended that you obtain a record of the number of responses to all alternative answers, and this will determine if a second alternative on the test items is not distinctive enough or too confusing for your students.

Another method for evaluation of these items, suggested by Reed Hunt and Henry Ellis, is to obtain a record of the number of the responses to each alternative answer given by students who scored in the top third of the class and in the bottom third of the class. This can be done by using a computer in large classes. The underlying assumption is that any individual item has validity if it correlates with the total score on the test. Instead of actually computing the correlation between the set of test scores and the scores of an individual item, one can obtain a good idea of the size of this correlation by comparing the class on the test as a whole. The validity of an item is supported if the proportion of the students in the top third of the class who answered the item correctly is substantially higher than the proportion answering correctly among the bottom third of the class. This is illustrated in the following example:

After information has been located by a search of the contents of long-term memory, it is gathered together and organized in:
    a. sensory memory
   *b. working memory
    c. the second level of processing
    d. the rehearsal buffer

PERCENTAGE OF STUDENTS
CHOOSING ALTERNATIVE

	a.	b.	c.	d.
TOP 1/3 STUDENTS	14	71	3	12
BOTTOM 1/3 STUDENTS	21	51	7	21

OVERALL PERCENT CORRECT = 62%

If the percentages responding correctly to alternative "b" had been reversed for the top and bottom thirds of the class, one could conclude that the item did not measure the same thing as the test as a whole and should question whether the question should be included on subsequent tests. Note that the information just given also allows the professor to calculate the relative difficulty of the item and which of the lures are perceived by students as plausible answers. If the overall performance on the test were 80 % correct, one might conclude that this item is more difficult than most and thus is useful in discriminating among people near the top of the class. For the hypothetical data just given, one might also conclude that answer "c" is detected by nearly all students as being incorrect and thus should probably be modified for future use.

Donna Frick-Horbury
Appalachian State University
Boone, NC

CHAPTER 1
INTRODUCTION TO COGNITIVE PSYCHOLOGY

A. KEY TERMS

cognitive psychology
perception
behaviorism
serial learning
introspection
stimulus-response
information processing
storage
cognitive neuroscience

psychophysics
structuralism
empiricism
creative synthesis
mechanism
computer model
output
linguistics
rationalism

B. DEMONSTRATIONS/STUDENT ACTIVITIES

1. THE PROBLEM OF KNOWLEDGE DEMONSTRATION

This demonstration is more in the form of a discussion topic, but usually works well to illustrate to students the idea of the problem of knowledge. Tell students the following story:

One day, this man named George was on his way to work, and he was stopped by a little old man in a white lab coat who explained that he was an inventor and that if George would let him try his invention out on him, he would pay a million dollars. The inventor explained that his invention was merely a machine that would make George dream and that it would not hurt him in any way. All that it would do is make George sleep, and for that he would get paid a million dollars. George decided that all he had to lose was one day's work and that he was going to do it, so the man took George into his laboratory and hooked him up to his machine, and George went to sleep. He dreamed that he was walking on the moon and that he had a date with one of the Spice Girls. Then he dreamed he was driving a Ferrari and was gambling in Monte Carlo. Then George woke up, and the inventor thanked him, paid him, and sent him home.

All the way home, George was thinking about what he was going to do with the money and how happy he and his wife would be. He walked in and said, "Hi honey, I'm home."

"You bum," she said, "You've been gone a year, and you prance in here like nothing."

A year! He could not believe it. How could he have been gone a year? All of a sudden, George wakes up, and the inventor is unhooking him from the machine. He thanks George, pays him and sends him home. All the way home, George is

1

thinking about what if he had really been gone a year, or two, or more. As he walks in the house, he hesitantly says, "It's me. It's George. I'm here, now."

"Hi, honey," his wife says, "How was your day?"

"You wouldn't believe it," George starts to explain, "I met this weird little man and."

And all of a sudden, George is back in the machine and the inventor is unhooking him. The question is, how do you know that this is reality and that you are not just hooked up to a machine somewhere dreaming all this?

Students typically have lots of reasons for telling you that they know that this is reality, but each of their claims can be questioned. Discuss this in terms of the book's statement that "what you really know is that a certain pattern of activity occurred in the brain."

2. PSYCHOPHYSICAL DEMONSTRATION OF PERCEPTION/METRONOME

This demonstration is suggested by the text on page 9-10 and it is simply to allow students to monitor the perceptual experience caused by a metronome set at one beat per second. Students will quickly see how the perception of rhythm occurs in a nonrhythmic stimulus. This experiment can be varied by having students open or shut their eyes, raise their hands when the perception begins to see if there is individual variability in this perceptual illusion, and change the timing of the metronome to determine if this changes the perception.

3. WEBER-FECHNER'S JND

An easy way to demonstrate "Just Noticeable Differences" is to fill two sets of five black film canisters with increasing numbers of heavy objects (ball bearings, marbles, bolts, fish weights). Mark the bottom of each canister concerning how many objects each contains. It is suggested that you increase each canister proportionally by 3, depending on which object you use. You should also label each canister on the bottom as Set 1; stimulus 1 through 5 and Set 2; S1- S5. Ask for a volunteer, and you can either blindfold the student or not. Ask them to hold out both hands palm up, and place one canister from each set on each hand. For example, in the right hand you place S2 from Set A and S2 from Set B in the left hand. Ask the student to weigh the two and determine that they are the same. Then pick up both canisters. Do not change the canister that is in the left hand, but change the right hand to S3, but do not let the student see what you are doing. Place both canisters simultaneously on each hand, then ask the student if they are the same of different. If they say different, ask which one has changed. If they cannot determine a change, repeat the procedure and change the stimulus by one increment. You can use the incremental presentation, which is the most simple but not as accurate as random presentation. Draw the following chart on the board, and test several students so that the class can see that perception varies per individual.

TRIAL	RIGHT HAND	LEFTHAND	RESPONSE	JND
TRIAL 1	STIMULUS 1	STIMULUS1	Equal	No
TRIAL 2	S1	S2	Equal	No
TRIAL 3	S1	S3	Left	JND =2

C. ADDITIONAL RESOURCES

1. Suggested Readings

Lachman, R., Lachman, J. L., & Butterfield, E. C. (1979). *Cognitive psychology and information processing: an introduction.* Hillsdale, N.J.: Erlbaum.

Neisser, U. (1967). *Cognitive psychology.* New York: Appleton-Century-Crofts.

Ornstein, R. (1997). *The evolution of consciousness: The origins of the way we think.* New York: Simon & Schuster.

2. Videotapes

The nature of memory. Films for the Humanities and Sciences.

The human quest: consciousness. Films for the Humanities and Sciences.

Through a glass darkly. Films for the Humanities and Sciences.

D. CHAPTER 1 TEST ITEMS

MULTIPLE-CHOICE

1. James and Wundt would both agree that crucial elements of cognition would include:
     (d). Page 8. Factual.

   a. intentionality

   b. creative synthesis

   c. volition

   d. both intentionality and volition

2. Weber and Fechner promoted the study of psychology by:
     (b). Page 6. Conceptual.

   a. providing mathematical formulas for brain activity which were used by neuroscientists for PET scans

   b. calculating a measurable relationship between environmental energy and psychological perception

   c. creating the research which became known as structuralism

   d. formulating an elementary theory of cognitive psychology based on the principle of creative synthesis

3. Structuralism is the position that:
     (a). Page 6. Factual.

   a. perception is a composite experience based on the elementary structural parts of the sensations

   b. the mind is comprised of three distinct structures; sensory register, short-term memory, and long-term memory

   c. an experience activates certain procedures which cumulatively structure a psychological event

   d. the mind is hierarchically organized from several structural elements

4. Parallel distributing processing is most similar to:
     (b). Page 26. Conceptual.

   a. mechanistic theory

   b. a computer model of information processing

   c. creative synthesis

   d. behaviorism

5. Computer models of the mind fail to be completely useful due to:
   (b). Page 27. Factual.

   a. their inability to promote empirical experiments

   b. their failure to include the concept of consciousness

   c. their inability to model sensory input

   d. none of the above; the computer model can accurately model mental operations of all facets

6. All of the following are similar in their proposals of mental models EXCEPT:
   (c). Page 6-25. Conceptual.

   a. mechanistic theory

   b. computer models

   c. structuralism

   d. cognitive neuroscience

7. The earlier psychophysical method of studying sensation was focused on:
   (d). Page 5-6. Factual.

   a. making a distinction between sensation and perception

   b. calculating a formula to measure consciousness

   c. discovering the structures of the mind

   d. establishing a correlation between physical energy and psychological processes

8. The importance of the psychophysical method was that it:
   (a). Page 6. Factual.

   a. allowed mental reaction to be quantitatively measured in response to varying levels of physical energy

   b. formulated a direct relationship between encoding and conscious experience

   c. allowed the entry of consciousness as an area of study

   d. demonstrated a connection between structures of the mind and mental processes

9. Analytical introspection is a:
   (c). Page 6. Factual.

   a. technique to enhance memory

   b. method of remembering long list of nonsense syllables

   c. procedure of analyzing a perception into elementary parts

   d. process of attending to all possible sensory information possible

10. Creative synthesis is an idea inherent in:
     (a). Page 7. Conceptual.

   a. structuralism

   b. information processing

   c. behaviorism

   d. mental models

11. Freud's idea of _____ is contained in many areas of current cognitive research.
     (d). Page 34. Factual.

   a. false memory syndrome

   b. defense mechanisms of threatening memories

   c. stages of cognitive development

   d. unconscious influences of prior experience

12. The difficulty encountered by the early mechanistic view was that:
     (b). Page 9. Conceptual.

   a. it did not have a mental model, such as the computer, to enable conceptualization of its hypothesis

   b. it could not explain emergent or synergistic perceptions, such as the tick tock rhythm of a clock

   c. it was difficult to test its predictions

   d. it could not account for processes such as attention, problem solving, or decision making

13. Behaviorism adapted the classical conditioning principles of reflex and association in order to accommodate:
     (a). Page 12. Factual.

   a. the processes of learning

   b. the principle of stimulus-response

   c. the question of knowledge

   d. the conscious/unconscious distinction

14. Although neobehaviorists and behaviorists differed on the acceptance of the ideas of motivation and learning, they shared the concept of the:
     (c). Page 14. Conceptual.

   a. principle of drive

   b. necessity of theory

   c. principle of stimulus-response language

   d. lack of the necessity of rigid scientific inquiry

15. One important contribution of the computer model is that it:
     (d). Page 21. Factual.

   a. focused on structuralism

   b. proposed mental vapors analogous to procedure

   c. reinforced the idea of empiricism

   d. provided a language to talk about cognitive processes

16. Cognitive psychology is the study of:
     (b). Page 23. Factual.

   a. motivation

   b. mental processes

   c. psychologists

   d. information

17. The reason that cognitive psychology is important is:
     (a). Page 23. Factual.

   a. mental processes are responsible for much of our behavior

   b. we can learn how language occurred in man

   c. the evolution of man is a cognitive process

   d. all of the above

18. A _____ is something which seems to function similarly to the object we are trying to understand.
     (c). Page 22. Factual.

   a. copy

   b. theory

   c. model

   d. structure

19. Historically, psychology began as a separate study of:
     (c). Page 32. Factual.

   a. physics

   b. history

   c. human knowledge and experience

   d. computer models

8

20. Analytical introspection is the process of:
     (a). Page 6. Factual.

   a. analyzing perceptions into elemental parts

   b. describing the structure of your mind

   c. identifying sensations from the environment

   d. all of the above

21. The beginning of cognitive psychology occurred when scientists began to develop theories of:
     (a). Page 21-22. Factual.

   a. human performance and attention

   b. short-term memory

   c. philosophy

   d. computer simulations

22. The _____ psychologists determined that the only proper topic of study for psychology was directly observable behavior.
     (d). Page 14. Factual.

   a. cognitive

   b. clinical

   c. social

   d. behavioralist

23. The current view of most cognitive psychologists is that the mind and mental processes are ways of describing _____ .
     (c). Page 25. Factual.

   a. motivation

   b. reasoning processes

   c. brain activity

   d. computer simulations

24. Solving problems through a combination of thinking and problem solving and data collection is known as:
     (b). Page 27. Factual.

   a. therapeutic design

   b. scientific method

   c. methodological procedure

   d. computer program

25. The procedure that psychologists use to study mental functioning is:
    (a). Page 27. Factual.

    a. get an idea or theory about how mental processes work and then set up an experiment

    b. look at the behavior and guess how it originated

    c. set up an experiment and see what happens, then devise a theory about it

    d. reproduce an experiment that has already been done

26. In studying animals, we sometimes infer that their reactions can be compared to human behavior. Therefore, we use the animal as a _____ for understanding the human.
    (c). Page 22. Conceptual.

    a. research idea

    b. guinea pig

    c. model

    d. structure and process

27. A _____ is something we already understand which functions similarly to something else that we are trying to understand.
    (c). Page 22. Factual.

    a. receptor

    b. idea

    c. model

    d. procedure

28. In the computer model, the storage function is analogous to human _____ .
    (a). Page 23. Factual.

    a. memory

    b. encoding

    c. energy

    d. output

29. The storage function of a computer is analogous to the process we usually think of as:
    (a). Page 23. Factual.

    a. memory

    b. input

    c. feedback

    d. information processing

30. The general framework of human processing and computer models is called:
    (b). Page 23. Factual.

    a. the Cheryl Tiggs model

    b. information processing

    c. psychologist framework

    d. behaviorism

31. The three components of cognition in information processing consist of:
    (c). Page 23. Factual.

    a. thinking, problem solving, and decision making

    b. conception, understanding, and verbalization

    c. input processing, storage, and output

    d. reading, writing, and arithmetic

32. Once a visual stimulus is perceived by a human, the sequence of information processing is:
    (a). Page 31. Factual.

    a. input processing, storage, and output processing

    b. visual recognition, attention, and identification

    c. visual and auditory matching, brain activity, and neural transmission

    d. muscle action, receptor action, and mental action

33. The input processes of information processing consists of:
    (b). Page 31. Factual.

    a. problem solving and reasoning

    b. pattern recognition and attention

    c. short- and long-term memory

    d. all of the above

34. The computer model has been criticized on the grounds that a computer cannot:
    (d). Page 35. Factual.

    a. talk and feel

    b. reason and remember

    c. create

    d. understand, perceive, or be conscious

TRUE FALSE

1. In the mechanistic view of the mind, energy activated sensory nerves, which in turn, activated a representation of prior experience tantamount to conscious experience.

    (true).

2. Intentionality, goals, and plans are mental phenomena that affect behavior.

    (true).

3. Ebbinghaus's nonsense syllable memory test was devised so that the capacity of long-term memory could be studied.

    (false).

4. Chomsky's position on language acquisition validated that of behaviorism by advocating that syntax and grammar are reinforced by the parent.

    (false).

5. Rats who were shocked for drinking water continued to drink it anyway because shock is not an environmental event which the rat is prepared to accept as an associated effect of taste.

    (true).

6. Fechner's just noticeable difference between two stimuli allowed for the mathematical calculation of sensory input and changes in perception.

    (true).

7. We have an equal number of successful cognitive operations and failures in cognitive functioning, but we tend to notice the failure more.

    (true).

8. Behaviorists thought that only overt behavior must be studied.

    (true).

9. In the sequence of information processing, the computer model suggests that both short-term and long-term memory are storage units.

    (true).

10. The input stage of processing consists of problem-solving and reasoning processes.

    (false).

11. Computers can understand in the same way that humans do.

    (false).

12. It has been shown that computers can demonstrate consciousness.

    (false).

13. If you had no memory of the past, you would not have any basis for predicting the future.

(true).

14. All models of science are usually ultimately right.

(false).

15. Sensory information is encoded directly into long-term memory.

(false).

ESSAY

1. Discuss the similarities and differences between creative synthesis and parallel distributed processing.

2. Behaviorism proposed that a thought is like a stimulus-response effect, while the information processing model proposes that given an appropriate cue for an event, a person retrieves a memory for that event. How are these two positions different?

3. How did cognitive psychology originate, and what does it typically study?

CHAPTER 2
PERCEPTUAL PROCESSES

A. KEY TERMS

sensory register	template
pattern recognition	serial processing
sensory trace	parallel processing
veridical	preprocessing
partial report technique	analysis-by-synthesis
whole report technique	features
backward masking	data driven
precategorical	presynthesis
echoic memory	connectionism
modality effects	geons
suffix effects	distributed knowledge
higher-order processing	parallel distributed processing
perceptual deficit hypothesis	feature detectors

B. DEMONSTRATIONS/STUDENT RESEARCH PROJECTS

1. MODALITY EFFECT AND THE SENSORY REGISTER

For this experiment, half of the class will have to leave the room for the auditory presentation of a list of words. In Handout 2-1, there is a list of 12 words. Tell the students that you are going to present them with a list of words one at a time. Do not tell them it is for a memory test. Read each word slowly, and at the end of the list, ask students to take out a piece of paper and recall the words in any order that they can remember. When they are finished, test the remainder of the class on the same words, but use a visual presentation, either slide presentation or overhead transparencies. Present the words at the same rate as the auditory presentation, and ask the subjects to recall the words in the same way. When completed, score the results of the recall test for both groups. Subjects in the auditory group should recall more of the last words of the list than subjects in the visual presentation group. Are there any differences in total recall between the two groups? If so, ask students to discuss why this might be so. Does enhancement for the last words of the list for the auditory group result in overall better performance, or just that the last words are better remembered.

2. FEATURE ANALYSIS AND VISUAL SEARCH

Students are given two lists of letters from Handout 2-2. Instruct them to keep the lists face down until told to start. At that time, they are to turn the first list over and search for the letter *Z* that is embedded in the list. As soon as they find it, they are to say "*stop.*" You can do this experiment with one or two subjects and use a stopwatch to time their search, or the whole class can participate and raise their hands when finished. When students have finished the first list, proceed with the second list in the same way.

Students will easily see that the search for the target letter is much easier and faster in the first list. Ask students why this is so in terms of feature theory and does this validate the assumption of parallel processing?

Adapted from Neisser, U. (1964). Visual search. *Scientific American, 210,* 94-102.

3. EIDETIC MEMORY OR PHOTOGRAPHIC MEMORY

Many students think that they have a photographic memory, and asking for a show of hands is very likely to reveal at least a few of the believers. Eidetic memory has been proposed to be visual in nature. Leask, Haber, and Haber (1968) described the phenomena as being "a visual image of a figure, usually long in duration, localized in space in front of the subject's eyes, positive in color and usually in the plane where the original figure was shown" (p.1). Very few people seem to display this trait, with only approximately 0.08% of the people tested. It also seems to be more particular in children than adults, and the eidetiker reports actually seeing the image floating in front of their visual field so that their remarkable recall of the image is not memory but simply reporting what they still can see of the iconic image. This phenomenon could be proposed as a dysfunctional sensory register whereby the iconic memory does not erase of decay. To test your students for their eidetic memory, show them the picture in Handout 2-3 and ask them to stare at the image for one minute and then to stare at a blank piece of gray paper or screen. Ask the following questions.

1. What do you see?

2. Is it an image floating in front of you or a mental image?

3. How many children are in the boat?

4. What is the little girl holding?

5. What kind of animal is on the beach?

6. How many animals do you see on the beach?

7. Can you see the stripes on the one turtle?

8. How many dark stripes are there?

9. How many large stars are in the sky?

10. How may fish are jumping out of the water?

11. Are there clouds in the sky?

12. What is in the little boy's hand? (nothing)

13. Is the boat dark or light?

14. What kind of tree is on the island?

15. How many coconuts are hanging from the tree?

HANDOUT 2-1

TEST ITEMS FOR MODALITY EFFECTS

1. SHARK	7. PAPER
2. MELON	8. CHAIR
3. LIGHT	9. DAISY
4. CAMEL	10. RANCH
5. OCEAN	11. APPLE
6. SHIRT	12. PLATE

SCORING FOR MODALITY EFFECT

Ask for a show of hands for the subjects in the visual presentation group who recalled the first word of the list. Then ask for a show of hands for subjects in the auditory group. Continue until all 12 words are scored.

	AUDITORY	VISUAL
1.		
2.		
3.		
4.		
5.		
6.		
7.		
8.		
9.		
10.		
11.		
12.		

Adapted from Conrad, R., & Hull, A. J. (1968). Input modality and the serial position curve in short-term memory. *Psychonomic Science, 10*, 135-36.

FEATURE ANALYSIS AND VISUAL SEARCH

LIST 1

BDRGUQ
UDROCG
QCOGUR
OQGBCS
ROQBSC
GQCSRD
CSOQJU
SBUOCR
GDCSQO
DCSOUR
UXOUCS
OCUSRD
CQOSDR
UCSQDO

LIST 2

EVWKMI
NWVLZE
ILKZME
HYEWZI
HNMTIW
WZLKMV
VWMNHI
VZKWYM
ZMVKYW
KYNWMN
VZKMXN
NZVMKW
WMZNIK
HWVMYN

EIDETIC MEMORY FIGURE

C. ADDITIONAL RESOURCES

1. Suggested Readings

Feldman, J. A., (1985). Connectionist models and their applications: Introduction. *Cognitive Science, 9,* 1-2.

Geyer, L. H., & DeWald, C. G. (1973). Feature lists and confusion matrices. *Perception and Psychophysics, 14,* 471-82.

Gibson, E. J. (1969). *Principles of perceptual learning and development,* New York: Prentice Hall.

Hintzman, D. L. (1990). Human learning and memory: Connections and dissociations. *Annual Review of Psychology, 41,* 109-39.

Lindsay, P. H., & Norman, D. A. (1977). *Human Information Processing* (2nd). New York: Academic Press.

Neisser, U. (1964). Visual search, *Scientific American, 210,* 94-107.

Neisser, U. (1967). *Cognitive Psychology.* New York: Appleton-Century-Crofts.

Selfridge, O. (1959). Pandemonium: A paradigm for learning. In *Symposium on the mechanization of thought processes.* London: HM Stationary Office.

Sperling, G. (1960). The information available in brief visual presentations. *Psychological Monographs, 74,* (Whole number, 498).

2. Videotapes

The enchanted loom: Processing sensory information. Films for the Humanities and Sciences.
Inside information: The brain and how it works. Films for the Humanities and Sciences.

D. CHAPTER 2   TEST ITEMS

MULTIPLE-CHOICE

1. In processing sensory information, it is thought that the sensory register is necessary because:
    (d). Page 40. Factual.

    a. of the time it takes to identify sensory information

    b. we need a buffer to hold information until it can be further processed

    c. it is assumed that we cannot process two sensory patterns simultaneously

    d. all of the above

2. In a laboratory room, you are in a soundproof booth, and your task is to hit a button every time you hear a tone played. Whenever the auditory signal occurs, your sensory register records and stores the signal in a _____ for further processing.
    (b) . Page 40. Conceptual

    a. holding matrix

    b. sensory trace

    c. processing activation mode

    d. auditory coding pattern

3. Which of the following is NOT a characteristic of the sensory register.
    (c). Page 40. Conceptual.

    a. Information is stored in a veridical form.

    b. Information is meaningless until further processing.

    c. The storage space for sensory information is small.

    d. The information lasts only a brief time.

4. In Sperling's experiment, a whole report consisted of naming:
    (a). Page 41. Factual.

    a. the letters of one row of the letter matrix that was indicated by a tone or marker

    b. off the letters from one of the rows of the letter matrix within a given time limit

    c. off as many letters as possible from the entire letter matrix

    d. off the bottom row only from the letter matrix

5. Which of the following was NOT a hypothesis made by Sperling concerning the sensory register.
     (c). Page 41-46. Conceptual.

   a. Information decayed off the sensory register before you could name more than four of the letters.

   b. Sensory information from the sensory register was veridical.

   c. Information was selected off the sensory register for further processing by the mechanism of attention.

   d. Information was held in sensory register for approximately 1/3 of a second.

6. In the sensory register, visual information is to auditory information as:
     (c). Page 45. Conceptual.

   a. feature is to template

   b. precategorical is to pattern recognition

   c. iconic is to echoic

   d. erasure is to decay

7. In an experiment with a letter matrix where the subject is cued for the recall of one specific letter rather than the whole line, the subject is first briefly shown the matrix and then cued with a circle placed in the location of the target letter. When the subject is asked to report the letter, they do not perform very well. This experiment is known as backward masking illustrates:
     (b). Page 42. Factual.

   a. that subjects have very poor memory for letter matrices

   b. that information on the sensory register is erased by new stimuli

   c. that information on the sensory register is meaningless

   d. that the sensory register holds the information verbatim for 1/3 second

8. One explanation of the suffix effect relies on the concept of _____ masking.
     (b). Page 46. Factual.

   a. forward

   b. backward

   c. visual

   d. subliminal

9. The sensory register has several characteristics, one of which makes pattern recognition absolutely necessary as a stage of processing information. This characteristic is:
     (c). Page 45. Conceptual.

   a. the large capacity it has for all sensory information

   b. its echoic memory trace

   c. its precategorical code

   d. the backward masking ability

10. Data from different kinds of studies are consistent in suggesting that the duration of visual sensory memory is approximately:
    (d). Page 43. Factual.

    a. 1/3 millisecond

    b. 3 milliseconds

    c. 30 milliseconds

    d. 300 milliseconds

11. In a backward masking experiment, if the cue marker (circle) used to indicate the target letter is presented after 300 milliseconds, then there are no effects of the mask. This indicates that:
    (c). Page 43. Conceptual.

    a. the letter has been erased

    b. the letter has been masked by the marker

    c. the matrix has decayed off the sensory register

    d. the marker is an ineffective tool to test with

12. When subjects are given a brief presentation of a matrix that consists of half letters and half numbers, and are asked to report just the numbers, they typically perform at the same level as a whole report. Since subjects are asked only to report part of the information, they should perform at a level close to 100%. The explanation for this performance deficit is that on the sensory register:
    (b). Page 44. Conceptual.

    a. these symbols are backward masking each other, since the symbols are not the same across the matrix

    b. these symbols are meaningless and have to be categorized, which takes more than 300 milliseconds

    c. the auditory instructions of "report the numbers" erases the visual information of the matrix

    d. the context speeds erasure for further processing, and the information is no longer available on the sensory register

13. Experiments performed on the auditory sensory register indicate that:
    (b). Page 45. Factual.

    a. both the visual and auditory sensory register are equivalent in all characteristics

    b. the echoic memory is longer in duration than the iconic memory

    c. auditory information on the sensory register has meaning

    d. people can recall auditory information off the sensory register for up to 10 minutes

14. When following a conversation, meaning and comprehension of the sentence is slower than the rate of speech. For this reason it is necessary that we have:
    (a). Page 45. Factual.

    a. an auditory sensory register

    b. a modality effect

    c. visual and auditory pattern matching

    d. pattern recognition prior to sensory register processing

15. Results from a study by Watkins and Watkins suggest that echoic memory may persist for at least _____ seconds.
    (c). Page 47. Factual.

    a. 0.20

    b. 2.0

    c. 20

    d. 200

16. Pattern recognition mainly serves to:
    (b). Page 48-51. Factual.

    a. erase backward masking effects off the sensory register

    b. add meaning to the sensory information

    c. differentiate between auditory and visual template matching processes

    d. increase the duration of information on the sensory register

17. The suffix effect occurs when:
    (a). Page 46. Factual.

    a. an additional word is added onto a list of to-be-remembered words as a signal for the end of the list

    b. the orthographic similarity of visually presented words interferes with memory for the last letters of a word

    c. there are several words in a list that end in "ed" or "ing"

    d. all of the above

18. The suffix effect can be contributed to:
    (c). Page 46. Factual.

    a. iconic memory which confuses similar words

    b. the recency effect

    c. backward masking in echoic memory

    d. the modality effect

19. The idea that we have a literal copy of all sensory stimuli in memory comes from the:
    (b). Page 53. Conceptual.

    a. suffix effect

    b. template theory

    c. lock-and-key hypothesis

    d. analysis-by-synthesis

20. Morrison presented groups of good and bad readers with an array of eight symbols and used an adaptation of Sperling's partial report procedure with a recognition test. Morrison's results showed that:
    (d). Page 49. Factual.

    a. the perceptual deficit hypothesis of specific reading ability was accurate

    b. the poor readers performed less well at all delayed recognition intervals

    c. there were no differences between good and poor readers at either immediate or any delayed recognition intervals

    d. poor readers performed as well as good readers at recognition intervals that permitted the information to remain in sensory memory.

21. The modality effect is when:
    (d). Page 47. Factual.

    a. the mode of information entering the sensory register interferes with duration of the information contained on the sensory register

    b. the length of time that the information is presented is a direct function of its ability to be recognized

    c. information has to be pattern recognized first, as numbers or letters, before it can be recalled

    d. a subject remembers the last few items of a word list better when they are presented auditorily than when they are presented visually

22. One of the primary problems with early template theory was:
    (d). Page 54-55. Factual.

    a. the wide variation of physical patterns

    b. the speed in which pattern recognition occurs

    c. the number of templates required for a lock-and-key match

    d. all of the above

23. One of the assumptions of analysis-by-synthesis is that:
    (d). Page 55. Factual.

   a. the comparison of the pattern of sensory information to the templates is a serial processing analysis

   b. pattern recognition is a data driven process

   c. the decision stage of pattern recognition is simply a frequency activation

   d. patterns of sensory information are represented by component features in memory

24. In an experiment by Neisser, it was demonstrated that it takes less time to spot a letter (Z) in a list of other dissimilar letters (O/U/B/Q) than it does to spot the letter in a list of similar letters (X/V/N/K). This experiment is used as evidence for which theory?
    (b). Page 54-58. Conceptual. (Is based on Handout)

   a. template theory

   b. feature theory

   c. pattern recognition theory

   d. alphabet theory

25. In an experiment by Neisser, subjects were required to scan a sheet of paper with 50 lines of 4 letters each for either a specific target letter of any one of ten different letters. The subjects perform similarly in both conditions. In terms of the template theory, this experiment is consistent with the idea that this type of pattern recognition demonstrates:
    (c). Page 63. Conceptual.

   a. conceptually driven processing

   b. serial processing

   c. parallel processing

   d. sensory register precategorical information

26. In feature theory, the memory component of sensory patterns is represented by:
    (a). Page 55. Factual.

   a. features

   b. orientations

   c. whole templates

   d. schemas

27. When a frog sitting on a lily pad sees a fly moving near him, he has a specific set of visual cells that respond to this specific pattern. This type of "lunch" detector seems to validate:
    (d). Page 55. Conceptual.

    a. template theory

    b. data-driven processing

    c. parallel distributed processes

    d. feature theory

28. In the process of analysis-by-synthesis, contextual information:
    (d). Page 57-66. Factual.

    a. facilitates expectations of probable patterns, which in turn expedites pattern construction

    b. narrows the list of potential candidates for pattern recognition

    c. presynthesizes the sensory pattern

    d. all of the above

29. Given a picture of a rabbit or a picture of a girl's face, subjects will write either *HARE* or *HAIR* depending on which picture they view. This is an example of:
    (d). Page 58. Conceptual.

    a. precategorical processing

    b. eidetic memory

    c. advertising bias

    d. conceptually driven processing

30. Overlooking the same typographical errors during four careful proofreadings of a manuscript illustrates the role of _____ in pattern recognition.
    (d). Page 58. Factual.

    a. stimulus overload

    b. pattern similarity

    c. parallel processing

    d. presynthesis

31. If you are told that you will be shown some pictures of animals, you might recognize a picture of an animal from an ambiguous sensory pattern that might not really be an animal at all. This type of pattern recognition whereby you construct a pattern based on expectation rather than sensory information is known as:
    (a). Page 58. Conceptual.

    a. presynthesis

    b. perceptual deficit hypothesis

    c. modality effect

    d. *dos equis* effect

32. Context, expectations, and priming can change the speed and response of pattern recognition due to:
    (d). Page 58. Factual.

    a. data-driven (bottom-up) processing

    b. the divided-attention effect

    c. limited processing capacity

    d. activating conceptual information (presynthesis)

33. The primary difference's in parallel distributed processing and earlier theories of pattern recognition is:
    (d). Page 63. Factual.

    a. that all processing occurs in parallel rather than any serial processing

    b. that instead of a computer as a model of pattern recognition, brain activity is a better representation

    c. the connections in neural networks are the result of learning and represent knowledge rather than storage residing primarily within a memory node

    d. all of the above

34. The structural theory of pattern recognition can account for:
    (b). Page 59. Factual.

    a. serial processing

    b. spatial relationships among features of an object

    c. geometrical as well as nongeometrical objects

    d. an infinite number of templates

35. Structural theory and pattern recognition theory differ only on the proposal that:
    (a). Page 59. Factual.

    a. there are 36 geons sufficient for all pattern recognition

    b. an object is recognized by analysis of component features of all objects

    c. all features are compared to a template stored in short-term memory

    d. none of the above, they share all of the above assumptions

TRUE FALSE

1. Each sensory modality has its own sensory register.

   (true).

2. Information stored in the sensory register is immediately changed to a form that is more similar to its stored template or features.

   (false).

3. Information on the sensory register decays within 300 milliseconds or is erased by new information.

   (true).

4. Information on the sensory register is precategorical until further processing.

   (true).

5. Backward masking works to speed the decay of information off the sensory register.

   (false).

6. The modality effect is where visual information interferes with memory for the last few items in a serial list of words.

   (false).

7. In pattern recognition, serial processing is faster on some tasks than parallel processing.

   (false).

8. Analysis-by-synthesis is a form of pattern recognition that matches the features of a physical pattern to features stored in memory for a best-fit recognition.

   (true).

9. The suffix effect seems to cause backward masking of the list item in echoic memory and interferes with memory for the last word.

   (true).

10. The ability to recall the last few items of a list better when the presentation is auditory rather than visual is known as the suffix effect.

    (false).

11. Both the modality effect and the suffix effect rely on echoic memory for explanation of their results.

    (true).

12. Morrison's experiment with poor and good readers indicates that the deficit for poor readers occurs while processing the information off the sensory register.

    (false).

13. Information on the sensory register is assumed to be precategorical while meaning is derived with the process of pattern recognition.

    (true).

14. In analysis-by-synthesis, pattern recognition can be either data driven or conceptually driven processing.

(true).

15. Parallel distributed processing assumes that there is a primary node that is activated during the process of pattern recognition.

(false).

ESSAY

1. Information on the sensory register has been said to both (1) decay and (2) be erased from the sensory register by new incoming information. How have these claims been verified by experiments?

2. How do both the modality effect and the suffix effect depend on echoic memory to explain their findings?

3. You are given the word *BOOK* and asked if it is a word. Explain the process of pattern recognition starting with the encoding of the word on the sensory register through the process of analysis-by-synthesis.

4. How does the principle of conceptually driven processing sometimes interfere with correct pattern recognition?

5. You are given a two lists of random letters. List 1 consist of letters such as *V W X K Y N Z*, and List 2 consist of letters, such as *O C S Q U B G*. Your task is to find the letter *M* that is embedded in each of the lists as fast as you can. According to feature theory, which list would you perform the fastest on and why?

6. At a very fast presentation rate, you are given a word and told to identify what the word is. The word that you are trying to identify is *BOOK*, but you are not sure what the last letter was. Compare and contrast what the analysis-by-synthesis approach would say about your processing to what the parallel distributed processing approach would say about your processing.

A. KEY TERMS

switch model	late-selection
pattern recognition	priming
attention	masking
early-selection	capacity
preconscious processing	secondary task
dichotic listening	automatic processing
shadowing	Stroop effect
attenuator	action slips
feature integration theory	subcortical attention system
posterior attention system	anterior attention system

B. DEMONSTRATION/STUDENT RESEARCH PROJECTS

1. DICHOTIC LISTENING TASK

Pick three students and assign two of them to be the readers and the third to be the listener. Give Handout 3-1 to the two readers and assign one passage to each reader. Have the readers practice reading the prose passage before class. They should be told to practice together, reading at approximately the same speed and loudness. The student who reads the second passage should fill in the blanks with appropriate personal information concerning the third student who will be doing the listening task.

Instruct the listener to concentrate only on passage 1 and ignore passage 2. Tell them that they will be asked questions about the first passage at the end. Seat the listener slightly in front of the two readers with about one foot distance on either side of the readers. Instruct the listener to look straight ahead. Give a start signal and allow the readers to read for about one minute before stopping them.

After the task, ask the listener what the first passage was about. Then ask if they can tell you anything about the second passage. They will be able to tell you something about both messages. Discuss this in terms of the predictions of the switch model and attenuator model.

2. PRIMING EXPERIMENT

This experiment illustrates to the students how one task can prime the system to process and respond in a predetermined manner. Simply ask the students to repeat the word *SILK* eight times as fast as they can. Then immediately ask them the question, "What do cows drink?" They will quickly respond *MILK* due to the rhyming priming and will not see their mistake that cows give milk and drink water. Even if you ask them a second time what cows drink, they will very emphatically give the same answer. Once you tell them the mistake, they find the experiment exciting.

3. STROOP EFFECT AND AUTOMATIC PROCESSING

The Stroop effect is easily demonstrated to the whole class by copying the materials from Handout 3-2 onto three large pieces of poster board. Print each list item in the color indicated on Handout 3-2. Ask for three volunteers and assign each student a first, second, and third position. Instruct the students to name the <u>color</u> that the word is printed in and ignore the written material itself. Tell them to name from the top to the bottom of the list <u>AS FAST AS THEY CAN</u>!

Tell the second and third persons that they can listen to the other person recite the colors, but they cannot see the other student's list. They are to turn their heads and not look until it is their turn. Emphasize once again that they are to do this task as rapidly as possible.

Give the first student their list so that the whole class can see the list. Then, test the second student in the same way. When the third student is given the list, he or she will try to keep the same pace as the first two students and, therefore, should automatically read the words and not name the colors. Discuss this in terms of reading as an automatic process.

HANDOUT 3-1

READING PASSAGE

This is a tricky question because language is not the same thing as communication. It seems likely that all animals have some form of communication with other members of their species. An interesting question in the animal world is whether or not animals have language so that they can talk to each other. Communication can be in the form of smell, visual displays of body postures and facial expressions, auditory cues that signal danger or other information, or even chemical messages that are passed from one member of a species to a second member. Without this type of communication within species members or between members of two different species, there would be very little harmony in the animal world.

However, language between animals implies a different sort of communication, where the information can be conveyed that portrays circumstances or environmental conditions. One animal that has been studied concerning its language behavior is the honeybee.

The honeybee is a social insect that forages for food in the area of its hive. If a honeybee finds a food source, it is very quickly aided by other bees of its hive to retrieve the food. How do the other members of the colony know exactly where the food is located? They know because the first honeybee to discover the food source communicates to the other members exactly how far and in exactly what direction they need to travel to find the food. It does this by displaying a pattern of flying outside of the hive that tells the other bees which direction to fly in and how far in relation to the sun. This is called the dance of the honeybee.

For example, if the food source is very near the hive, the bee only dances in a series of small circles, first in one direction and then reversing to the other direction. If the food source is further away, the bee will do a waggle dance consisting of a figure-eight pattern. The waggle occurs during the middle portion of the figure-eight pattern. If the dance occurs outside of the hive, the waggle part points directly toward the food. The duration of the waggle pattern indicates distance to the other hive members. The longer the waggle, the farther the food. The bees also emits a series of buzzing sounds during this dance which is also thought to communicate other information. It is not known exactly how the auditory signal is used, but generally it is thought that it is a redundancy within the system which communicates information that is consistent with the dance language.

READING PASSAGE

College life is not always easy. The student is usually leaving home for the first time and making a new, independent life for themselves. They have to make new friends, live in strange dormitories, find their way around a new town, and meet the requirements of classes and professors. The demands are sometimes very hard, but there are also fun times that make up for the hardships.

For example, (name) had to leave (his/her) hometown of (city) , and come to (city of university), in (state) to attend (name of university) . At (university), (name) was a (psychology ?) major. They worked very hard and made good grades until they took a psychology class on Human Learning and Memory with Dr. (name). This class was very hard, although

33

(name) volunteered for several experiments to pull up (his/her) grade. (Name) really hoped for an A out of the course.   (Name) also enjoyed going to parties, movies, and football games. The football team was known as the (name).

The school colors were (colors), but today (name) wore a (color) outfit. This just goes to show that sometimes (name) and college life do clash.

The campus at (university) is very pretty. There are several gardens that are available for students to go and sit in and think. Sometimes students have picnics there. The food at this school is generally pretty good also. There is the cafeteria on campus, or else there are several local eating places where students hang out. One of these is named   (name) . The students can go and have a hamburger or just a coke. It is always crowded. (Name) eats there often and has been known to be the center of attention on several occasions.

The campus itself is centrally located between the towns of (town) and (town) . The nearest airport is about   (distance) miles away. Most students do not fly home for the semester break but either get a ride from someone or else do not go home at all but rather go to (town of resort). Here there is a great gathering of students to celebrate the fall or spring break from college life. It is this type of fun that makes college life bearable. Our next semester break is in (number) weeks. I wonder whether or not (name) is going home or headed toward a vacation spot? Whichever it is, I am sure that they will be studying for their human learning and cognition class the whole time.

HANDOUT 3-2

LIST 1

STIMULUS	COLOR TO BE PRINTED IN
NHE	GREEN
SGG	BLUE
LSY	YELLOW
PRW	BLACK
WRT	RED
GAB	PURPLE
KHG	BLUE
QBC	YELLOW
LHJ	GREEN
CMN	RED
HDN	PURPLE
DGB	BLUE

LIST 2

STIMULUS	COLOR TO BE PRINTED IN
GREEN	GREEN
BLUE	BLUE
YELLOW	YELLOW
BLACK	BLACK
RED	RED
PURPLE	PURPLE
BLUE	BLUE
YELLOW	YELLOW
GREEN	GREEN
RED	RED
PURPLE	PURPLE
BLUE	BLUE

LIST 3

COLOR TO BE PRINTED IN

STIMULUS	COLOR TO BE PRINTED IN
GREEN	GREEN
BLACK	BLUE
PURPLE	YELLOW
BLUE	BLACK
YELLOW	RED
RED	PURPLE
GREEN	BLUE
BLUE	YELLOW
RED	GREEN
YELLOW	RED
PURPLE	PURPLE
BLACK	BLUE

36

C. ADDITIONAL RESOURCES

1. Suggested Readings

Cherry, R. S., & Kruger, B. (1983). Selective auditory attention abilities of learning disabled and normal achieving children. *Journal of Learning Disabilities, 16,* 202-05.

Dawson, M. E., & Schell, A. M. (1983). Lateral asymmetries in electro-dermal responses to nonattended stimuli: A reply to Walker and Ceci. *Journal of Experimental Psychology: Human Perception and Performance*, 9, 148-50.

Johnston, W. A., & Heinz, S. P. (1978). Flexibility and capacity demands of attention. *Journal of Experimental Psychology*, 107, 420-35.

Lewis, J. L. (1970). Semantic processing of unattended messages using dichotic listening. *Journal of Experimental Psychology, 85,* 225-28.

Logan, G. D. (1990). Repetition priming and automaticity: Common underlying mechanisms? *Cognitive Psychology, 22,* 1-35.

Mackay, D. G. (1973). Aspects of the theory of comprehension, memory and attention. *Quarterly Journal of Experimental Psychology, 25,* 22-40.

Mowbray, G. H. (1953). Simultaneous vision and audition: The comprehension of prose passages with varying levels of difficulty. *Journal of Experimental Psychology, 46,* 365-72.

Palmer, J. (1990). Attentional limits on the perception and memory of visual information. *Journal of Experimental Psychology: Human Perception and Performance, 16,* 332-50.

2. Videotapes

Information processing, (1971). CRM/ MacGraw-Hill Films, 110 Fifteenth St., Del Mar, CA.
Inside information: The brain and how it works. Films for the Humanities and Sciences
The study of attention. Films for the Humanities and Sciences.

D. CHAPTER 3   TEST ITEMS

MULTIPLE-CHOICE

1. According to Broadbent's early-selection filter theory of attention, if you have an intense phone conversation while a movie is playing on the TV, your knowledge of the movie will consist of:
(b). Page 73. Conceptual.

    a. nothing, you will not be aware at all of the TV

    b. the physical characteristics of the TV movie, such as the sex of the actor

    c. limited semantic knowledge-just enough to have a limited idea of the movie's plot

    d. complete semantic knowledge, assuming you can watch the TV and hear your phone conversation

2. What theory of attention is LEAST flexible in allowing us to do more than one task at a time?
(a). Page 71. Conceptual.

    a. early-selection filter theory

    b. late-selection filter theory

    c. attenuator theory

    d. capacity theory

3. For both early-selection models of attention, the proposed mechanism for selection of the material to be processed is:
(c). Page 72. Factual.

    a. priming

    b. semantic meaning

    c. physical/sensory saliency

    d. data-driven demands

4. Broadbent's early-selection model operates on the principle of:
(b). Page 72. Factual.

    a. disuse hypothesis

    b. all or none

    c. graded potential

    d. divided attention

5. Which theory of attention does not allow for the concept of preconscious processing?
     (a). Page 80. Factual.

    a. early-selection switch model

    b. late-selection filter theory

    c. Marcel's semantic priming

    d. capacity model of attention

6. Moray found that subjects did recognize that their names had been uttered in the nonattended ear during shadowing. Why does this cast doubt on Broadbent's theory of attention?
     (c). Page 74. Conceptual.

    a. A person's name is too large to fit on the sensory register.

    b. The filter must have known that the person's name was coming up and switched channels to the unattended ear.

    c. He predicts that the switch mechanism is only guided by physical properties of the auditory message and not processed for meaning.

    d. A name should be precategorically processed at the sensory register stage of information.

7. Shadowing is a procedure which:
     (d). Page 73. Factual.

    a. predicts that auditory information processing follows visual processing

    b. allows that the louder or brighter a stimulus, the more likely it is to get selected for further processing

    c. determines that lower levels of physical stimulus will be discarded by selection processes

    d. requires a listener to repeat verbatim a message presented to one ear and disregard the second

8. In using the procedure of shadowing, you are assured that:
     (d). Page 73. Factual.

    a. subjects do not switch attention to another channel of information

    b. if subjects switch attention to an unattended channel, the shadowing task will be disrupted

    c. attention is focused only on one message

    d. all of the above

9. Studies of dichotic listening tasks show that:
     (b). Page 73. Factual.

    a. nonshadowed material is not processed for any meaning

    b. nonshadowed material is processed for some meaning

    c. shadowed material is not processed for meaning

    d. shadowed and nonshadowed material do not differ in degree of meaningful processing

10. Treisman's attenuator model suggested that:
      (b). Page 74. Factual.

   a. attention operates like a mechanical on/off switch

   b. different amounts of information can come through more than one channel at the same time

   c. pattern recognition for an unattended message cannot occur

   d. processing information does not depend on attention, but rather the operation of the sensory register

11. In a dichotic listening task, Treisman presented a semantic message that began in the shadowed ear and continued in the nonshadowed ear. Subjects followed the meaning of the message and not the physical location of the message. This suggests that subjects are processing the unattended message for meaning. This experiment led Treisman to formulate the attenuator model. This model is:
      (b). Page 74-77. Factual.

   a. a late-selection model of attention

   b. a modified version of Broadbent's theory

   c. a semantic priming theory of memory

   d. a preconscious model of processing

12. The primary difference between early and late-selection models of attention is that early-selection theories predict that we select what we are going to attend to before further processing, while late-selection predicts:
      (c). Page 80. Factual.

   a. selection of response will be limited to semantic information

   b. semantic processing will occur immediately but attention is restricted to later preconscious processing

   c. that all messages will activate meaning, but a response to two different messages will not be possible

   d. the system will select the input and the response output early in the process so as to expand capacity

13. On a lexical decision task when subjects are given a list of words some of which are preceded with a related word such as *DOCTOR - NURSE*, the related second word had a shorter reaction time than an unrelated word. This is known as:
      (b). Page 78. Factual.

   a. lexical reaction time

   b. semantic priming

   c. capacity limitations on decision tasks

   d. late-selection activation

14. In a semantic priming task, Marcel gave subjects a triplet of words such as *TREE - PALM - WRIST* and tested for lexical reaction time to the third word. He found that even if a priming word was pattern masked so that the subject was unaware of its presentation, it still facilitated lexical decision time. Marcel concluded:
    (c). Page 78. Factual-Conceptual.

    a. that attention occurred early in the information processing selection sequence

    b. masking the second word increased arousal and thus speeded reaction time

    c. that masking a word did not disrupt the priming effect because this occurred at a preconscious level

    d. masking the first word would have resulted in the same performance levels as masking facilitates speed of processing.

15. Which of the following statements best describes the findings of Marcel's semantic priming experiment?
    (d). Page 79. Factual.

    a. Attention, pattern recognition, and consciousness are components of one process that have no limitations on selection or response.

    b. When a word is primed by a semantically related word, all of these activations are available to consciousness, and the system chooses which activation is the most appropriate.

    c. Early-selection filter models are the most valid in describing how pattern recognition and attention function.

    d. Pattern recognition and meaning occurs at a preconscious level, while attention is restricted to selecting among the activated meanings and responding consciously to only one interpretation.

16. Marcel's semantic priming experiment validates which theory?
    (c). Page 79. Factual.

    a. Broadbent's switch model

    b. Treisman's attenuator model

    c. late-selection model of attention

    d. capacity model of attention

17. According to the capacity model of attention, under what conditions would our performance on a primary task decline?
    (d). Page 81-82. Conceptual.

    a. whenever we try to do a secondary task

    b. whenever the primary task requires the recognition of more than one input

    c. whenever we try to do a secondary task that requires more cognitive resources than we have available

    d. Both a and c are correct.

18. In Marcel's experiment, a congruent word primes the speeded response for a target word, but an incongruent prime only facilitates the response if it is pattern masked. This curious finding is explained in the context of all late-selection model, and that is that:
    (c). Page 79. Factual.

    a. the unmasked word primes in the direction of the associated semantic meaning, such as tree, palm, _coconut_

    b. conscious attention has preselected the possible target and thus demonstrates that attention occurs after pattern recognition

    c. the mask prevents conscious processing of the primed word and thus all associated meanings, congruent or incongruent, are activated for future selectivity

    d. all of the above

19. If a task has become automatic, this implies that this task:
    (a). Page 83. Factual.

    a. requires little central capacity resources

    b. is controlled by the posterior attention system

    c. in now available for conscious monitoring

    d. all of the above

20. The theory which predicts that attention requires some, if not all, of our limited processing resources is known as:
    (c). Page 81. Factual.

    a. Marcel's semantic priming theory

    b. Treisman's attenuator model of attention

    c. Kahneman's capacity model of attention

    d. Posner's processing model of attention

21. In the capacity model, attention involves a decision to:
    (a). Page 81. Factual.

    a. allocate processing resources

    b. block unattended material before pattern recognition

    c. block unattended material after pattern recognition

    d. remain inflexible

22. Which of the following is NOT a prediction of capacity models of attention?
   (c). Page 81-82. Conceptual.

   a. The requirement of two simultaneous tasks may exceed our processing resources.

   b. We are able to perform two tasks at once if we do not exceed capacity, but requirements from Task 1 are summed with requirements from Task 2, and if this exceeds capacity, then performance will decrease on one or both tasks.

   c. Given two tasks which exceeds capacity, it is always the performance on the secondary task which is decreased.

   d. Allocation of processing resources is flexible.

23. One important process that allows the system to perform two tasks at once without exceeding processing resources is that of:
   (a). Page 84. Factual.

   a. automaticity

   b. arousal

   c. attention

   d. effortful processing

24. That you can drive a car and carry on a conversation with a passenger at the same time best illustrates:
   (a). Page 84. Conceptual.

   a. automaticity

   b. attention

   c. the role of sensory register

   d. Japanese engineering

25. The primary determinant of automaticity is:
   (c). Page 84. Factual.

   a. the material

   b. the other tasks required at the same time

   c. the amount and kind of practice of the activity

   d. genetic

26. Posner's experiment on lexical decision (is A = A) demonstrated that:
   (d). Page 84. Conceptual.

   a. rehearsal of a letter requires resource capacity

   b. decision tasks processes take a great deal of capacity

   c. recognition of letters is automatic

   d. all of the above

27. In Posner's lexical decision task (is A = A?), the task that required the greatest amount of processing resources was:
   (a). Page 84. Conceptual.

   a. the decision process of matching the second letter to the first

   b. the reading of the first letter

   c. the rehearsal of the first letter until the second letter presentation

   d. the processing of the warning tone for letter presentation

28. Logan's theory of automaticity proposes that:
   (c). Page 86-87. Factual.

   a. automatic responses are a result of repeated activation of the neural circuitry so that they retain a residual excitation at all times

   b. automatic behaviors are simply a function of reduced response time

   c. all actions require a rule for performance, but well-practiced outcomes are part of memory for the event, and the solution rule is no longer required

   d. automatic responses occur in the more primitive subcortical areas of the brain and, therefore, require less attentional resources

29. In Posner's lexical decision task (is A = A?), capacity requirements of the primary task were measured by:
   (b). Page 84. Factual.

   a. the correct yes/no response to the letter matching

   b. the reaction time to a secondary task of responding to a tone

   c. the reaction time of lexical decision of whether the letters match

   d. a recall test of which letters had matched during the task

30. One of the primary findings of Posner's lexical decision experiment was that:
   (c). Page 84. Factual.

   a. letter matching requires a great deal of capacity

   b. letter matching requires too much capacity to perform a secondary task

   c. recognition of letters requires very little capacity and is therefore an automatic process

   d. such a low effort task of letter matching is not sufficient to test capacity

31. The primary argument of the Feature Integration Theory is that:
   (d). Page 89. Factual.

   a. primitive features of an object are subjective to parallel processing

   b. processing of the features of an object is automatic

   c. integration of an object's features requires serial processing and therefore, attention

   d. all of the above

32. In a modified Stroop test, Kahneman and Treisman present an array which gives both relevant and irrelevant information for processing. In this case, the Stroop effect does not occur. They conclude:
(d). Page 88. Factual.

a. attention filters out irrelevant information

b. perception of an object's properties (color, size, etc.), are automatically processed

c. object discrimination is a capacity-consuming, attentional task

d. all of the above

33. The neurocognitive theory of attention proposed by Posner suggests that the system that would direct attention spatially is the:
(b). Page 91. Factual

a. subcortical attentional system

b. posterior attentional system

c. anterior attentional system

d. all of the above are required for full attention

34. Concerning the complex relationships among perception, attention, and consciousness, which of the following is true.
(d). Page 93. Factual.

a. Early-selection theory was wrong.

b. Late-selection theory was wrong.

c. Capacity theory was wrong.

d. Al three positions have merit and validity.

35. Broadbent's switch theory of attention would be consistent with the proposed function of the _____ in Posner's neurocognitive theory of attention.
(a). Page 91. Conceptual.

a. subcortical attentional system

b. posterior attentional system

c. anterior attentional system

d. all three are required for full attention

TRUE FALSE

1. If you are paying attention to a very hard task, there is no capacity left over for attending to a secondary task.

   (false).

2. Attention can be defined as the decision to allocate processing resources.

   (true).

3. Capacity theories predict that we have a limited amount of processing resources to allocate to different tasks.

   (true).

4. It takes a large amount of capacity to input information from the sensory register.

   (false).

5. Preconscious processing could be said to be very similar to, or the same as, subliminal perception.

   (true).

6. A dichotic listening task is where a subject simultaneously shadows two auditory messages for meaning.

   (false).

7. The switch model of attention predicts that we can switch attention back and forth between two messages as a function of the meaning involved in the messages.

   (false).

8. Treisman's attenuator model is a modification of Broadbent's early-selection model of attention.

   (true).

9. The most important factor in promoting automaticity seems to be attention.

   (false).

10. In early-selection models of attention, the criterion for selecting what to attend to is physical or sensory saliency.

    (true).

11. It is assumed that semantic priming occurs due to the spreading activation of one related word to another.

    (true).

12. In late-selection models of attention, selection occurs at input.

    (false).

13. The Stroop effect is the decrease of reaction time to a secondary task when the primary task requires most of the capacity.

    (false).

14. Marcel interpreted the results of his lexical decision experiment in terms of preconscious processing.

    (true).

15. Normal functioning of the frontal lobes which results in normal behavioral actions is a result of both excitation and inhibition of schemas appropriate to the general situation.

    (true).

ESSAY

1. Compare and contrast the early- and late-selection models of attention.

2. What is the relationship between early- and late-selection filter models and the capacity model, and how does research illustrate this position?

3. How does the concept of automaticity validate the capacity theory?

4. In a shadowing experiment (Lewis, 1970), subjects were given a list of words in one ear and a separate list of words in the nonshadowed ear. Some of the words in the nonshadowed ear were synonyms of the words in the shadowed ear. When this happened, the rate of verbal shadowing was slower than when the words were not synonyms. How would early-selection filter models deal with these findings? How would late-selection models explain these results?

5. Kahneman's allocation policy states that attention is controlled by enduring dispositions for involuntary attention, momentary task intentions, evaluation of capacity demands, and the degree of arousal. Discuss the conscious or unconscious aspects of these factors in the context of Posner's neurocognitive theory where there are three attentional systems.

CHAPTER 4
SHORT-TERM MEMORY, WORKING MEMORY

A. KEY TERMS

primary memory	serial position effect
secondary memory	primacy effect
stage model	recency effect
control processes	anterograde amnesia
rehearsal	implicit memory
coding	explicit memory
trace life	central executive
articulatory loop	working memory
storage capacity	visuo-spatial workpad
interference	rote rehearsal
maintenance rehearsal	elaborative rehearsal
chunking	fragment completion
spatial-delayed response test	phonological loop

B. DEMONSTRATIONS/STUDENT ACTIVITIES

1. SHORT-TERM MEMORY CAPACITY

To demonstrate to students the capacity of short-term memory, ask them first to estimate from within a range of 0 to 25 how many items they think they can remember immediately after their presentation. Students will usually greatly overestimate their capacity. To test their short-term memory capacity, tell them you will say the word *TEST* to alert them for the upcoming items, then they will hear the items, and when you say the word *WRITE* they are to write down the items in the same order as they heard them.

NOW! 749	WRITE THE NUMBERS.
NOW! 9375	WRITE THE NUMBERS.
NOW! 36710	WRITE THE NUMBERS.
NOW! 067268	WRITE THE NUMBERS.
NOW! 5814072	WRITE THE NUMBERS.
NOW! 361747130	WRITE THE NUMBERS.
NOW! 1638328024	WRITE THE NUMBERS.
NOW! 38603159603	WRITE THE NUMBERS.

2. CHUNKING

To demonstrate that chunking helps increase memory capacity, tell students that you are going to give them three lists of letters and test how many letters they can remember. Call out the letters at a normal speed with the same amount of time between each letter (you might need to practice this). Use the procedure of calling out an alert word, such as *NOW*, call out the letters, then instruct the students to write the letters. Have students count the number of letters they recalled. Then repeat for Test 2 and 3. For Test 3, the letters should be called out as you normally would for the three-letter acronym.

Test 1 primes the students to expect similar results as when testing short term memory. Test 2 serves as a baseline for memory without chunking. Test 3 illustrates that the same material as in Test 2 can be remembered perfectly when chunked into meaningful units.

<u>TEST 1</u>   NOW! H T K C Q L P B S M Z D   WRITE THE LETTERS.

<u>TEST 2</u>   NOW! P H D B M W I B M C I A   WRITE THE LETTERS.

<u>TEST 3</u>   NOW! PHD BMW IBM CIA   WRITE THE LETTERS.

3. PRIMACY AND RECENCY EFFECT

This exercise is designed to demonstrate several aspects of memory performance simultaneously, including the primacy and recency effects, the difference between recall and recognition memory, and even the difference in recall between concrete and abstract words. Although the distinction between recall and recognition is not made until chapter 6, you can have students label their memory tests for future reference, or make the point here.

In Handout 4-1, there are two lists of words. The first list consist of the target recall list. Call out the words, and ask the students to write down each word. At the end of the list, tell the students to cover the words they just wrote and get out a clean sheet of paper. Then ask them to write down as many words as they can remember, *IN ANY ORDER*. Ask them to label this sheet Recall Test and give them about five minutes to work. Ask them to count the number of words that they recalled. Then tell the students to cover up those words so that they cannot see them and that you are going to call out a new list of words. Use List 2 on Handout 4-1. If they recognize the words from List 1, they are to write it down. At the end of the recognition list, ask them to count the number of words they recognized.

Ask how many students recalled more words than they recognized. Discuss this in the context of recall and recognition memory or wait until Chapter 6 to discuss this aspect of memory. To demonstrate the primacy and recency effects, ask the students to look at their recall list and to circle the words if they recalled: *SNOW,   FRICTION,   TRAIN,   PARALLEL,   ILLEGAL, ELEPHANT, JUSTICE, FLOWER*. Ask them to count the number of circles and calculate a ratio of those words out of the total 16 words. You can also ask them to count the remaining 8 words from the middle of the list and calculate a ratio. You should have a majority of students who show a primacy and recency effect. Discuss this in the context of the store model or Baddeley's working memory. In addition, the odd numbered words are concrete and the even numbered words are abstract. There should also be an advantage for the concrete words. Abstract and concrete are discussed in chapter 5.

HANDOUT 4-1

WORD LIST 1- RECALL

1. SNOW
2. FRICTION
3. TRAIN
4. PARALLEL
5. STRAW
6. LOVE
7. PENCIL
8. SCIENCE
9. FIRE
10. DEVELOP
11. SOFA
12. VALOR
13. FLOWER
14. JUSTICE
15. ELEPHANT
16. ILLEGAL

WORD LIST 2- RECOGNITION

1. MOUSE
2. CABOOSE
3. SLASH
4. PENCIL
5. COFFEE
6. JUSTICE
7. REPEAT
8. RECORD
9. SNOW
10. FIRE
11. TRANSPIRE
12. SKIRT
13. FRICTION
14. SWIRL
15. TRAIN
16. TULIP
17. SOFA
18. EXPIRE
19. ELEPHANT
20. MARCH
21. PARALLEL
22. ILLEGAL
23. NUMBER
24. FLOWER
25. DEVELOP
26. WHEEL
27. PERIOD
28. STRAW
29. VALOR
30. WATER
31. LOVE
32. SCIENCE

C. ADDITIONAL RESOURCES

1. Suggested readings:

Baddeley, A. D. (1963). A Zeigarnik-like effect in the recall of anagram solutions. *Quarterly Journal of Experimental Psychology, 18,* 302-09.

Cohen, N. J., & Squire, L. (1980). Preserved learning and retention of pattern analyzing skill in amnesics: Dissociations of knowing how and knowing that. *Science, 210,* 207-10.

Craik, F. I. M., & Watkins, M. J. (1973). The role of rehearsal in short-term memory. *Journal of Verbal Learning and Verbal Behavior, 12,* 599-07.

Graf. P., & Schacter, D. L. (1985). Implicit and explicit memory for new associations in normal and amnesic subjects. *Journal of Experimental Psychology: Learning, Memory and Cognition, 11,* 501-18.

Milner, B. (1970). Memory and the medial temporal regions of the brain. In K. H. Pribram & D. E. Broadbent (Eds), *Biology of Memory.* New York: Academic Press.

Moscovitch, M. (1982). Multiple dissociations of function in amnesia. In L.S. Cermak (Ed.), *Human Memory and Amnesia.* Hillsdate, N.J.: Erlbaum.

Schacter D. L., & Tulving, E. (1982). Amnesia and memory research. In L. S. Cermak (Ed.), *Human memory and amnesia.* Hillsdate, NJ: Erlbaum.

Warrington, E. K., & Weiskrantz, L. (1978). Further analysis of the prior learning effect in amnesic patients. *Neuropsychologia, 16,* 169-76.

2. Videotapes

Brain series- Learning and memory. PPS Film Services, 1320 Braddock Place, Alexandria, VA.
Memory- The past imperfect. Films for the Humanities and Sciences.

CHAPTER 4   TEST ITEMS

MULTIPLE-CHOICE

STM = short-term memory
LTM = long-term memory

1. In STM, rehearsal serves the two functions of:
   (c). Page 99. Factual.

   a. encoding information off of the sensory register and coding it into LTM

   b. reducing the size of the memory unit and increasing the capacity of STM

   c. retaining information in STM as long as needed and transferring it to LTM

   d. focusing attention to the information and relating it to other semantic facts

2. One way of increasing the duration of STM is through the process of:
   (b). Page 103. Conceptual.

   a. sensory register integration

   b. rehearsal strategies

   c. chunking

   d. pattern recognition

3. Which type of memory has limited storage capacity and frequently involves acoustic encoding?
   (a). Page 102-104. Factual.

   a. short-term memory

   b. iconic memory

   c. state-dependent memory

   d. episodic memory

   e. procedural memory

4. Duncan used to be very absentminded in remembering people's names. Now when he is introduced to someone, he repeats their name over and over to himself. This strategy is known as:
   (c). Page 103. Factual.

   a. chunking

   b. automatic processing

   c. rehearsal

   d. state-dependent memory

5. STM is characterized by all of the following EXCEPT:
   (d). Page 102. Factual.

   a. small capacity

   b. rehearsal capabilities

   c. processing from information off the sensory register

   d. semantic memory

6. The capacity of STM is on the average:
   (b). Page 103. Factual.

   a. 9 items

   b. 5 to 9 items

   c. 15 chunks

   d. dependent of the type of information

7. In the Brown-Peterson paradigm, the purpose of presenting subjects with a number from which they counted backward by threes was to:
   (c). Page 108. Conceptual.

   a. promote numerical manipulation

   b. facilitate rehearsal of the to-be-remembered items

   c. minimize rehearsal of the to-be-remembered items

   d. confuse the subjects as much as possible

8. Typical results from a Brown-Peterson experiment suggest that subjects remember only 10 % of the material after:
   (a). Page 108. Factual.

   a. 18 seconds

   b. 118 milliseconds

   c. 30 seconds

   d. 68 seconds

9. One reason that information may be forgotten is because new information may be presented between the presentation of the to-be-remembered event and the recall test. This is known as:
   (a). Page 108. Factual.

   a. interference

   b. rehearsal prevention task

   c. trace life disintegration

   d. sensory register interception

10. Which of the following involves relating to-be-remembered information to other facts one already knows?
    (c). Page 103. Factual.

    a. rehearsal

    b. rote rehearsal

    c. elaborative rehearsal

    d. maintenance

11. One way of increasing the capacity of STM is through the process of:
    (c). Page 104. Conceptual.

    a. maintenance rehearsal

    b. encoding

    c. chunking

    d. rote rehearsal

12. The term *chunking* refers to:
    (d). Page 104. Factual.

    a. adding weight to an idea by the process of elaboration

    b. the integration of all sensory information about an event in order to make it meaningful

    c. coding information visually, acoustically, and semantically to make certain of LTM transfer

    d. the organization of discrete items of information into larger units

13. If you are given a pair of words such as *HORSE - MUSTACHE*, you might make an image of a horse with a big mustache. This is known as:
    (d). Page 103. Conceptual.

    a. attentional rehearsal

    b. rote rehearsal

    c. maintenance rehearsal

    d. elaborative rehearsal

14. The neurocognitive model of short-term memory tends to indicate that:
    (d). Page 113. Factual.

    a. sensory information is encoded and stored in parallel in the same anterior location of the brain

    b. the sensory register is located in the sensory areas of the brain, while short-term memory functions activate higher cortical areas

    c. all of the neural firing occurs in parallel so that the store model is invalid

    d. information is permanently stored in the posterior areas of the brain, while a typical STM retrieval task activates neurons in the frontal lobe

15. If you are given a sequence of 12 letters to remember such as *PHDBWMIBMCIA*, this will exceed the capacity of STM. However, if you group the letters so that it reads *PHD, BWM, IBM,* and *CIA,* you will have no trouble remembering them. This is due to the process of:
    (c). Page 194. Conceptual, based on demonstration 2.

    a. coding in LTM

    b. rehearsal readiness

    c. chunking

    d. STM pattern detection

16. The memory code for STM is thought to be based on:
    (b). Page 104. Factual.

    a. semantics

    b. acoustics

    c. genetics

    d. sensory input specificity

17. The greater likelihood of an item's retrieval when its serial position is near the end of the list refers to
    (b). Page 10 5. Factual.

    a. its control processes

    b. its recency effect

    c. its primacy effect

    d. both b and c

18. At the end of the class period, the student remembered the material of the last few minutes of class and the first material in class, but not the material in the middle. What is the term used to explain this:
    (c). Page 105. Conceptual.

    a. first and last recall

    b. situation irony

    c. serial position effect

    d. secondary memory recall

19. According to the Store model the reason for the primacy and recency effect is that the first material is stored in _____ , while the last material is processed in _____, and the middle material has not been encoded.
    (a). Page 106. Conceptual.

    a. STM; LTM

    b. LTM; STM

    c. sensory register; STM

    d. semantic; episodic

20. STM has previously been proposed to be associated with attention and consciousness. This is consistent with recent neurocognitive research which shows that:
    (d). Page 113-114. Conceptual.

    a. a STM task activates the frontal lobe

    b. the frontal lobe is where the highest level of attention is based

    c. STM is basically a high-level form of attention

    d. all of the above

21. Marylyn has a client coming to dinner at her house, but she is delayed at work and cannot get to the grocery store. She calls her husband and tells him to get: crackers, cheese, lettuce, carrots, onions, cucumbers, wine, steaks, cheesecake, asparagus, potatoes, and butter. Jeffery does not write the list down. Which part of the dinner is most likely not going to be served?
    (b). Page 103. Conceptual.

    a. salad and appetizers

    b. meat and dessert

    c. vegetables

    d. appetizers and vegetables

22. The Brown-Peterson paradigm illustrates that:
    (d). Page 101. Factual.

    a. information in STM is subject to decay

    b. STM has a very brief trace life so that 90% of the material is lost after 18 seconds

    c. there are different principles in forgetting between STM and LTM

    d. all of the above

23. What are the primary reasons for forgetting in STM?
    (d). Page 101-103. Factual.

    a. decay

    b. interference

    c. not processing information because it was not attended to

    d. all of the above

24. When amnesic patients are given a list of words to study followed by a fragment completion test which includes the wordstems of the original words, they perform just as well as normal subjects. This indicates that:
    (b). Page 110. Factual.

    a. there is a problem in transferring information from STM to LTM

    b. there is a problem in conscious, or effortful retrieval

    c. amnesiacs have been diagnosed wrong

    d. normal people have problems with stem-completion task

25. The idea of working memory has a controlling, decision-making mechanism is known as the:
    (a). Page 115. Factual.

    a. central executive

    b. implicit processor

    c. articulatory loop

    d. primary

26. The primary function of the visuo-spatial sketch pad in working memory is:
    (c). Page 116. Factual.

    a. in order that visual information can be processed off of the sensory register

    b. to rotate objects visually in space

    c. to store and manipulate visual and spatial information

    d. to integrate auditory information with visual or spatial information

27. The concept of a working memory can account for:
    (a). Page 115-116. Conceptual.

    a. active and inactive states of memory

    b. conscious states of attention and retention

    c. the neurocognitive theory of attention

    d. the duration and capacity of sensory register

28. The word length effect in memory is the demonstration of:
       (b). Page 114. Factual

   a. increased memory for longer words

   b. decreased memory for longer words

   c. primacy effect for the longest words

   d. recency effect for the longest words

29. Baddeley's working memory is very similar to the:
       (a). Page 115. Factual.

   a. capacity models of attention

   b. early-selection models of pattern recognition

   c. analysis by synthesis

   d. feature integration model

30. In working memory, the two subsystems are thought to be:
       (b). Page 116. Factual.

   a. used only when capacity is exceeded

   b. modality specific work spaces

   c. primarily a buffer for speech rehearsal

   d. a hierarchical capacity system which allows the performance of a secondary task when the primary task requires most of the processing resources

31. The central executive is responsible for:
       (c). Page 118. Factual.

   a. encoding, storage, and retrieval processing

   b. taking information from sensory register and transferring it to STM

   c. allocation of capacity for task demands

   d. the interaction of STM and LTM neural networks

32. The current view of the STM and LTM storage system is:
       (d). Page 119. Factual.

   a. that they are two distinct storage systems of memory

   b. deficits in STM can be overcome by the LTM store

   c. STM and LTM are hierarchically organized

   d. that STM is a process which interacts with processes in LTM

33. Mary had to remember a list of objects, such as light, mug, and automobile. When she was later given a recall test, the words that were recalled were not the original, but rather, lamp, cup, and car. The reason that this happens is that Mary encoded the words:
    (a). Page 104. Conceptual.

   a. semantically

   b. visually

   c. acoustically

   d. automatically

34. If given a list of word pairs to remember, the best performance can be achieved by:
    (d). Page 93. Factual.

   a. rote rehearsal

   b. serial processing

   c. parallel processing

   d. elaborative processing

35. The tendency to immediately recall the first and last items in a list better than the middle items is called:
    (c). Page 105. Factual.

   a. proactive interference

   b. sequential processing

   c. serial position effect

   d. retroactive interference

TRUE FALSE

1. Rehearsal helps by extending the trace life of information in STM, but the help comes at the expense of capacity.

    (true).

2. Conscious processing and attention are concepts associated with STM.

    (true).

3. The primary concept of information processing is that information moves in stages through different structural units.

    (true).

4. The storage capacity of STM is limited to semantic information only.

    (false).

5. One of the most important control processes in STM is rehearsal.

    (true).

6. Brown and Peterson demonstrated that most information decays from STM within 18 seconds unless the subject uses rehearsal processes.

    (true).

7. One of the main reasons for forgetting in STM is interference.

    (true).

8. In STM, interference and decay are basically the same processes.

    (false).

9. Elaborative rehearsal is the process of slowly repeating items in STM in order to transfer information to LTM.

    (false).

10. An item is considered a *chunk* if it is restricted to less than 10 letters or numbers.

    (false).

11. Chunking serves to extend the trace life of STM.

    (true).

12. Rehearsal is a technique that allows you to retain information in STM indefinitely but to the extent of using up most of the recourse capacity.

    (true).

13. STM is an acoustic or phonetically based code.

    (true).

14. The recency effect is the tendency of material to be remembered better the more frequently it is presented to the subject.

   (false).

15. The articulatory loop is a process in STM which allows the verbal words to be pronounced correctly.

   (false).

ESSAY

1. Explain primacy recency effect in the context of Baddeley's concept of working memory.

2. Explain the serial position effect in terms of the three memory systems.

3. In short-term memory, the capacity is about seven items, and the duration of holding information is no more than 18 seconds. How can these limitations of the memory system be changed by purposeful control processes, and why do these techniques work?

CHAPTER 5
ENCODING IN LONG-TERM MEMORY

A. KEY TERMS

encoding
retrieval
retention
elaboration
congruity effect
distinctiveness hypothesis
organization
material-induced organization
clustering in recall
subjective organization
levels of processing
reality monitoring

self-relevance
generation effect
tip-of-the-tongue
imagery
mental travel
concrete
abstract
dual-code
verbal codes
imaginal codes
propositional code
mnemonics

B. DEMONSTRATIONS/STUDENT ACTIVITIES

1. REALITY MONITORING

Ask the students if they think they can always determine the difference between reality and dreams. They will definitely feel that they can. Tell the students that you are going to demonstrate that they cannot always discriminate between events that have actually occurred and events they have imagined. They will find this difficult to believe, and if asked to predict how accurate they are in determining the difference between reality and imagination, they will predict 95 to 100%.

Make a transparency from Handout 5-1. This can easily be made into a slide presentation or can be used on an overhead as long as only one word at a time is visible. Ask the students if they can imagine your voice saying a word out loud. Ask them to imagine you saying the word *PSYCHOLOGY*. It is important to get them to practice imagining your voice. Instruct the student that as each word is presented you will read the word out loud. After a 2-second pause, you will say *WRITE* and they are to write the word. If a word is presented that is preceded with an *, you will not say the word, but they are to imagine you pronouncing the word out loud, again after a 2-second pause, you will say *WRITE,* and they are to write it down also.

At the end of the presentation, they are to fold the written list so that they cannot see the words. You will call out each of the words, in order, and they are to number each word and write *REAL* if they think you called the word out or *IMAGINED* if they think they thought the word.

After they determine their answers, have each student score their own data. Pass out the matrix in Handout 5-2. Then call out each of the 40 words as to whether they were real or imagined. Have them check each word in the proper matrix. For example, as word number one was a real word, if students said that they imagined it, they would place a mark in the third cell of the matrix under *REAL/WRONG*. If the student said that it was real, they would place a check in the first cell of the matrix under *REAL/RIGHT*.

At the end of the list, each cell can be given a percentage of performance by dividing the number of marks in each cell by 40. Average scores are shown in parentheses in Handout 5-2.

2. IMAGERY EFFECTS ON MEMORY

In Handout 5-3, there is a list of word pairs. Divide the students into two groups, and tell them that you want to demonstrate the difference in memory performance between written and verbal instructions. Do not tell them you are going to demonstrate the effects of imagery.

Assign one group to the verbal instructions and the other group to the written instructions. Tell them that the written instruction group can hear the other group's instruction but that the verbal group cannot see the written instructions.

Say to the verbal group, "I am going to call out a list of word pairs and you are to silently verbally rehearse the pair of words. For example, if I say *FISH - RIBBON*, you are to repeat the pair of words *'FISH-RIBBON, FISH-RIBBON*, etc.' until the next pair of words. You are not to write the words down."

Tell the verbal group not to look while you write the instructions for the written group on the board. Instruct the written group, "Make a mental image of the two objects together. For example, *FISH-RIBBON*, make an image of a fish with a big ribbon tied around its tail".

Call out the word pairs to both groups, and allow about eight seconds between each pair. When the list is finished, ask the students to take out a sheet of paper and tell them that you will call out the first word of each pair, and they are to fill in the second word of each pair. Do not call them out in the same order as they were presented.

After the cued recall test, tally the number of target words recalled for each person of each group. The verbal recall group will do very poorly, but the imagery group will score close to 100%. Discuss this in terms of imagery, elaboration, and distinctiveness.

3. GENERATION EFFECTS ON MEMORY

Handout 5-4 has a list of word pairs with the first word in each pair consisting of a category topic and the second word a member of that category (*FISH-GUPPY*). All of the category words are complete words. One-third of the member words are complete (these are referred to as Read words), and the other two-thirds are fragments the student has to fill-in (*FISH-G_PP_*). One-third are easy fragment completions and require low amounts of effort to generate the answer (Easy words). The remaining one-third are difficult fragment completion words and require more effort in processing to answer (Hard).

Instruct the students to get a clean piece of paper. Tell them that you will be showing them a pair of words. The first word is a category topic, and the second word is a member of that category. Tell them that some of the second words are fragments, and they are to complete the word if they can and write it down. If they do not figure it out within 10 seconds, you will give them the answer and they are to then write it down. Warn them that some of the words are not fragments but whole words. They are also to write those words.

Make a transparency of the list and present one pair of words at a time, either on an overhead or a slide presentation for 10 seconds. Be careful not to reveal the answers at the time of presentation. Have a practice session first so that students clearly understand the procedure.

At the end of the generation phase, have students fold their papers so that they cannot see the words they wrote down. Tell them they are going to have a recall test and that you will cue them with the category word for each pair, and they are to recall the paired member word. Have them number each word, and give them 10 seconds per word for recall.

After the recall, score the data by calling out which group each word was in (Read, Easy, and Hard) and the correct answer. Have students count the number of words for each group that they recalled correctly. The order of recall should demonstrate that generated words are best recalled depending on the effort that went into processing and that the READ words were poorly recalled. Discuss these findings in the context of levels of processing, organization, and generation effects.

4. SEMANTIC ORIENTING TASK

In this task, students are given one of two lists of the same word pairs. The lists differ only on the instructional task to the students. List 1 asks the student to circle the object in the pair of words that is the largest. List 2 asks the student to circle the word out of the pair of words that is the longest. Students in the first group will be forced to semantically process the information, while the second group will perform only a shallow process.

Divide the students in half, preferably the right and left half of the room. Give half the students the first list of word pairs in Handout 5-5 and the other half the second list Handout 5-6. Tell the students to keep the paper turned over until you say, "go," at which time they are to turn the paper over, and as fast as they can, follow the instructions at the top of the page. When they are finished, they are to turn their papers face down.

When the students are all finished, tell them to keep their papers turned face down, and give the students a cued recall task by calling out the first word of each pair. Ask the students to write down the word corresponding to the cue. At the end of the list, ask for a show of hands of the number of students that recalled 15 to 20 of the words. There will be a great number of students in the semantic group and none from the nonsemantic group. Tell the students that both groups had the same words, and ask what they think the reason was for the differences in performance. Discuss this in terms of levels of processing and imagery as an elaborative cue.

HANDOUT 5-1

REALITY MONITORING

<u>PRACTICE SET</u>

EXAMINATION
COGNITION
*MEMORY
SEMANTIC
*REALITY
*MUSIC

REALITY MONITORING TEST

1. GLASS
2. *SENSATION
3. COMPACT
4. DREAM
5. *CLOUD
6. MACHINE
7. *GERMS
8. *CANDLE
9. *STUDY
10. KETCHUP
11. CHILDREN
12. FINGERS
13. RAILER
14. NORMAL
15. TEXTBOOK
16. *SCHOOL
17. *CAFETERIA
18. *MASSIVE
19. *MUSTARD
20. *SUMMER

21. SOAP
22. *PEAR
23. *WINDOW
24. *TURKEY
25. MARKET
26. UMBRELLA
27. BISCUIT
28. AIRPLANE
29. *STUDENT
30. *CLOCK
31. *HAMMER
32. *INSTRUMENT
33. *GENETIC
34. TOWEL
35. *MONEY
36. TYPEWRITER
37. *COFFEE
38. NECKTIE
39. PARROT
40. SWING

HANDOUT 5-2

SCORE SHEET FOR REALITY MONITORING TEST

Place a mark for each word in only one of the four cells.

	REAL	IMAGINED
RIGHT	(55%)	(53%)
WRONG	(40%)	(45%)

HANDOUT 5-3

WORD PAIRS FOR IMAGERY EXPERIMENT

<u>CUE WORD</u> <u>TARGET WORD</u>

CUE WORD	TARGET WORD
TRAIN	PAINT
JELLY	CORK
SNAKE	CARPET
JET	OCEAN
CANARY	TRUNK
GERM	SHOVEL
WORM	NEEDLE
BUCKET	TREE
CAVE	FOOTBALL
TOWEL	MIRROR
SCARF	OYSTER
PIANO	ALLIGATOR
FLEA	CARROT
LIBRARY	GARDEN
MOTH	DRESS
STOVE	DESK
FROG	DISHES
FIRE	TUNNEL
BANK	BICYCLE
PEBBLE	SLINGSHOT

HANDOUT 5-4

GENERATION EFFECT

PRACTICE SET

CATEGORY		TARGET	ANSWER
INSTRUMENT	-	CA_CU_AT_R	EASY/CALCULATOR
ANIMAL	-	C__C_D__E	HARD/CROCODILE
FOOD	-	BANANA	READ/BANANA

TEST SET

CATEGORY		TARGET	ANSWER
MINERAL	-	PYRITE	READ/PYRITE
JEWEL	-	E__R_D	HARD/EMERALD
BEVERAGE	-	EG_N_G	EASY/EGGNOG
COUNTRY	-	R_MA__A	EASY/ROMANIA
FRUIT	-	NECTARINE	READ/NECTARINE
REPTILE	-	I__A_A	HARD/IGUANA
FLOWER	-	C_N_I_N	HARD/CARNATION
COLOR	-	INDIGO	READ/INDIGO
SPORT	-	AR_H__Y	EASY/ARCHERY
CANDY	-	G__D_P	HARD/GUMDROP
TREE	-	JUNIPER	READ/JUNIPER
DOG	-	L_BR_D_R	EASY/LABRADOR
HERB	-	OR_G___	HARD/OREGANO
SONG	-	LU_L_B_Y	EASY/LULLABY
DIRECTION	-	FORWARD	READ/FORWARD
VEGETABLE	-	P_T_T_	EASY/POTATO
INSTRUMENT	-	A__O_D__N	HARD/ACCORDION
DIRECTION	-	FORWARD	READ/FORWARD
FURNITURE	-	STOOL	READ/STOOL
VEHICLE	-	T__I_A_	HARD/TAXICAB
SHAPE	-	T_I_N__E	EASY/TRIANGLE

TEST ITEMS FOR SEMANTIC ORIENTING TASK

LIST 1

CIRCLE THE OBJECT IN EACH PAIR OF WORDS THAT IS THE LARGEST.

FLOWERPOT - DESK

FOOTBALL - CAR

RANCH- MUSTACHE

ELEPHANT - PEACH

CAT- TIGER

SOFA - MOUSE

SADDLE - COCONUT

OYSTER - ASPARAGUS

GARDEN - WORM

LAMP - RING

ENVELOPE - PEN

HAMMER - CAVE

BELT - SHOVEL

CHURCH - BRIDE

SCARF - SHIRT

WATCH - FORK

COMB - LAMPSHADE

FLOOR - PLATE

SEASHELL - BOAT

VASE - HOUSE

TEST ITEMS FOR SEMANTIC ORIENTING TASK

LIST 2

<u>CIRCLE THE WORD IN EACH PAIR OF WORDS, THAT IS THE LONGEST.</u>

FLOWERPOT - DESK

FOOTBALL - CAR

RANCH- MUSTACHE

ELEPHANT - PEACH

CAT- TIGER

SOFA - MOUSE

SADDLE - COCONUT

OYSTER - ASPARAGUS

GARDEN - WORM

LAMP - RING

ENVELOPE - PEN

HAMMER - CAVE

BELT - SHOVEL

CHURCH - BRIDE

SCARF - SHIRT

WATCH - FORK

COMB - LAMPSHADE

FLOOR - PLATE

SEASHELL - BOAT

VASE - HOUSE

C. ADDITIONAL RESOURCES

1. Suggested Readings

Bower, G. H., & Gilligan, S. G. (1979). Remembering information related to one's self. *Journal of Research in Personality, 13,* 420-32.

Erdelyi, M. H., & Kleinbard, J. (1978). Has Ebbinghaus decayed with time? The growth recall (hypermnesia) over days. *Journal of Experimental Psychology: Human Learning and Memory, 4,* 275-89.

Frost, N. (1972). Encoding and retrieval in visual memory tasks. *Journal of Experimental Psychology, 95,* 317-26.

Gardiner, J. M., & Rowley, J. M. (1984). A generation effect with numbers rather than words. *Memory and Cognition, 12,* 443-45.

Gardiner, J. M., Craik, F. I. M., & Bleasdale, F. A. (1973). Retrieval difficulty and subsequent recall. *Memory and Cognition, 1,* 213-16.

Hunt, R. R., & Elliot, J. M. (1980). The role of nonsemantic information in memory: Orthographic distinctiveness effects on retention. *Journal of Experimental Psychology: General, 109,* 49-74.

Johnson, M. (1985). The origin of memory. In *Advances in cognitive-behavioral research and therapy* (Vol. 4). NJ: Academic Press.

Slamecka, N. J., & Fevreiski, J. (1983). The generation effect when generation fails. *Journal of Verbal Learning and Verbal Behavior, 22,* 153-63.

2. Videotapes

Inside information: The brain and how it works. Films for the Humanities and Sciences.
The study of memory. Films for the Humanities and Sciences.

D. CHAPTER 5 TEST ITEMS

MULTIPLE-CHOICE

1. In long-term memory, it is thought that forgetting is due to:
      (d). Page 124. Factual.

   a. decay of information

   b. erasure of information

   c. lack of sufficient storage space

   d. retrieval failure

2. When Bryon was in high school, he took a course in algebra and made an A in it. Since then, he has taken many other courses but none in math. Bryon was recently given an aptitude test which had some algebra problems on it, but he could not remember how to work any of the problems. In terms of long-term memory, what most likely happened was:
      (c). Page 124. Conceptual.

   a. the other courses that he had taken had crowded out the old knowledge and it no longer existed

   b. since the information had not been used in years, it decayed

   c. the information is still there, but retrieval failure has occurred since the cues were insufficient to retrieve the memory

   d. more current learning had erased the memory of algebra

3. Elizabeth Loftus showed subjects a scene of a man reading a book with a green cover. Before she tested their memory of this event, she suggested to the subjects that the book was a different color. Later, she found that if the subjects did not actually remembered the real color, they recalled the suggested color as having actually occurred. This suggests:
      (b). Page 123. Factual.

   a. that subjects have a permanent memory of the event but can be persuaded to report what the experimenter suggests

   b. that events that intervene between the real event and memory retrieval can modify or replace the original memory

   c. subjects have poor memory for colors, but excellent memory for events

   d. there was no problem in encoding the event, but retrieval was delayed by the intervening information

4. Studies in autobiographical memory have suggested that:
      (c). Page 123. Factual.

   a. events are remembered very well for up to 6 years, events over 6 years old have a 50% chance of being recognized

   b. people and events are poorly remembered, but facts are well retained

   c. retention of autobiographical events is very good

   d. it is dependent on the emotional content of the memory

5. In 10 years, you are most likely to have forgotten:
      (d). Page 123. Factual.

   a. the faces of over 60% of your classmates

   b. all of the foreign language that you learned as a freshman

   c. real-life events that occurred to you

   d. none of the above, you are likely to remember most of these events

6. A semantic orienting task is where subjects are:
      (a). Page 136. Factual, based on demonstration 4.

   a. given a list of words and asked to perform some task that would make them attend to the meaning of the words

   b. asked how several words are grouped together according to similarity in meaning

   c. asked to mentally visualize an object

   d. given a list of words for memorization in a special order

7. In an experiment on the congruity effect, which of the following sentences are you most likely to later recall the capitalized word?
      (a). Page 130. Factual.

   a. Is a DOG an animal?

   b. Is a STONE an animal?

   c. Is a DOG a stone?

   d. none of the above, you are just as likely to recall any of the above sentences

8. The reason for the congruity effect is:
      (c). Page 130. Factual.

   a. that only congruent sentences are semantically processed

   b. that only incongruent sentences are semantically processed

   c. congruent sentences result in more elaborate processing

   d. false sentences cause inappropriate associations in memory and result in recall of the wrong item

9. Levels of processing would predict that chunking the letters *E M R A I A R G* into the word *MARRIAGE* would result in better memory because of:
    (a). Page 128. Conceptual.

    a. semantic processing

    b. shallow processing

    c. intent to remember

    d. working memory

10. According to the distinctiveness hypothesis, _____ cues are usually better for memory because they are unique and, therefore, distinctive in specifying the to-be-remembered event.
    (b). Page 131. Factual.

    a. sensory

    b. semantic

    c. nonsemantic

    d. associated

11. Two groups of subjects are given a list of words such as PROCESS, DATA, LABORATORY. The first group, known as Group 1, is asked to rate the pleasantness of the words, while Group 2 is asked to pronounce the words differently than normal according to the stressed syllable. Later, both groups are asked to recall the words. Levels of processing theory would predict that:
    (c). Page 131. Conceptual.

    a. Group 1 and Group 2 would have similar levels of recall

    b. Group 1 would remember the words with high pleasantness rates better than words with low pleasantness rates

    c. Group 1 would recall more words than Group 2

    d. Group 2 would recall more words than Group 1

12. Two groups of subjects are given a list of words such as PROCESS, DATA, LABORATORY. The first group, known as Group 1, is asked to rate the pleasantness of the words, while Group 2 is asked to pronounce the words differently than normal according to the stressed syllable. Later, both groups are asked to recall the words. In this experiment, distinctiveness hypothesis would predict that:
    (a). Page 131. Factual.

    a. Group 1 and Group 2 would have similar levels of recall

    b. Group 1 would remember the words with high pleasantness rates better than words with low pleasantness rates

    c. Group 1 would recall more words than Group 2

    d. Group 2 would recall more words than Group 1

13. Which of the following is NOT a component of the distinctiveness hypothesis?
    (d). Page 131. Factual.

    a. A memory trace is a by-product of attention and pattern recognition.

    b. Nonsemantic information can be just as effective as semantic information in cueing memory.

    c. Distinctive cues are good for memory because they are unique to the memory event.

    d. Retrieval is a function of remembering the shared features among items to be remembered.

14. During an experiment, the class was given a list of word pairs. Half of the class was instructed to circle which of the words in the pair were longer, while the other half of the class was told to tell which of the items were larger. This is known as:
    (d). Page 126. Factual.

    a. short-term memory

    b. recall and recognition test

    c. imagery technique

    d. semantic orienting task

15. During an experiment, the class was given a list of word pairs. Half of the class was instructed to circle which of the words in the pair were longer, while the other half of the class was told to tell which of the items were larger. The reason that the second group had better memory was that this group had to:
    (d). Page 126. Applied.

    a. remember semantic information

    b. spend more time and energy processing

    c. pay attention to the meaning and form an image

    d. all of the above

16. You are given two lists of word pairs. In the first list, you are to determine which of the two objects in the pair are larger, and in the second list. you are to determine which of the two words has the most letters in it. Later, you are given a recall test of the two words. Which of the two lists are you going to recall the best, and in terms of levels of processing, why is there a difference? The primary difficulty for the original levels-of-processing hypothesis was:
    (c). Page 134. Factual.

    a. nonsemantic processing normally leads to better memory than does semantic processing

    b. orienting tasks really do not control encoding

    c. nonsemantic information does not decay more rapidly   than does semantic information

    d. semantic information is usually less distinctive than is nonsemantic information

17. A consistent ordering in the output of *unrelated* items in a list for memory is referred to as:
        (c). Page 134. Factual.

    a. material-induced organization

    b. elaboration

    c. subjective organization

    d. distinctiveness

18. The method used for measuring subjective organization in recall of a list of unrelated items is known as:
        (a). Page 134. Factual.

    a. consistency of output order

    b. recall output

    c. learning curve

    d. organizational matrix

19. In terms of organizational processes, both Mandler and Tulving agree that organization occurs at encoding, but Tulving states that the benefits of organization is more important to:
        (b). Page134. Factual.

    a. storage

    b. retrieval

    c. learning

    d. accessing and activation of memory

20. Distinctiveness is to organization as _____ is to _____.
        (a). Page 132. Factual.

    a. uniqueness, similarity

    b. encoding, storage

    c. features, properties

    d. related, unrelated

21. The relationship between distinctiveness and organization suggests that:
        (b). Page 134. Factual.

    a. neither are very important to memory

    b. both are important to memory

    c. organization is more important to memory

    d. distinctiveness is more important to memory

22. Two groups of people are given a list of personal adjectives. One group is asked to rate how descriptive the words are of themselves, while the second group rates the words for pleasantness. Later, both groups are given a recall test. The results show that:
(c). Page 134. Factual.

a. both of these groups recall the words similarly

b. the group that rates the pleasantness recalls more words

c. the more descriptive the word was of a person, the more likely they were to recall it

d. the more masculine adjectives were recalled better by the self-descriptive group

23. You are given a list of words and word fragments and are asked to write the words and complete the fragments. If you are then given a recall test, you are most likely to:
(c). Page 137. Factual, based on demonstration 3.

a. recall only the complete words

b. recall only the word fragment you were able to solve

c. recall more of the word fragments than whole words, regardless of whether you solved them or not.

d. there is no difference in performance between words or fragments.

24. The ability to better recall information that you generated rather than information given to you is known as the:
(a). Page 137. Factual.

a. generation effect

b. process productivity

c. self-production hypothesis

d. egocentric memory hypothesis

25. Glisky gave subjects both words to read and word fragments to complete at both a study session and a test session so that memory could be tested for these conditions. The following matrix represents this experiment:

T		STUDY	
E		**READ**	**GENERATE**
S	**READ**	0.10%	0.50%
T	**GENERATE**	0.30%	0.80%

What conclusions can be drawn concerning these findings?
(d). Page 138. Conceptual.

a. Reading a word at either study or test results in poorer memory than a generate condition.

b. generating a word at the study session results in better memory at a study session regardless of whether the word is read or generated at test session.

c. Generating a word at both study and test session results in the best memory performance.

d. all of the above

77

26. Glisky gave subjects both words to read and word fragments to complete at both a study session and a test session so that memory could be tested for these conditions. Subjects did best on the generate conditions and particularly when the study session and test session were both congruent and the subjects had to generate the word fragments. This outcome suggests that:
    (a) Page 138. Factual, and also based on the chart in question 25.

    a. it is the generation process that aids memory, not the generation memory trace

    b. it is the structural trace of the generation representation that produces better memory

    c. generation is a form of organization that produces better memory

    d. reading an item produces less activation of memory than generating an item

27. In the generation effect, when a subject is unable to generate the correct answer, memory performance:
    (b). Page 137. Factual.

    a. is poorer for the not-generated words than for read words

    b. is better for the not-generated words than for read words

    c. is good only for the words that were generated

    d. are equally good for read and not-generated words

28. In generation effect experiments where the subjects suffers generation failure, he still has a better recall for the generation attempts than for read words. This finding is good evidence that:
    (d). Page138. Factual.

    a. distinctiveness hypothesis is valid in this context

    b. reading a word does not produce a memory trace unless it is within a context

    c. generating and reading a word produce different structural networks

    d. it is the process of trying to generate that is crucial to memory.

29. According to levels of processing, given the target word UMBRELLA, which of the following tasks would result in deeper processing?
    (b). Page 142. Conceptual.

    a. How many vowels are in the word?

    b. Does it fit in the sentence, "The _____ protected them from the rain."

    c. Does the word rhyme with rock?

    d. Write the middle letter/s of the word.

30. Which of the following words are you most likely to remember best on a memory test?
    (c). Page 142. Conceptual.

    a. chaos, development, friction

    b. sadness, joy, depression

    c. telephone, cat, clock

    d. justice, briefcase, lawyer

31. Paivio's dual-code theory predicts that:
    (b). Page 142. Factual.

    a. there is a double visual code in memory that gives analogue representation and mental images

    b. there is a verbal code and imaginal code in memory

    c. there are two different storage spaces in memory, one for verbal and one for images

    d. all of the above

32. If you are trying to remember a written list of grocery items, you can either memorize the words or make an visual image of each of the items. According to Paivio's dual-code theory, you would most likely remember all the items best if you:
    (d). Page 142. Conceptual.

    a. memorized the words

    b. visualized the items

    c. memorized the words in alphabetical order

    d. both memorized the words and visualized the items

33. What is the central belief of the dual-code theory?
    (b). Page 143. Factual.

    a. Knowledge goes through two stages or codes before it is stored.

    b. We have two different kinds of memory-- visual and verbal. Each is based on its own code.

    c. Visual memories are simply an elaboration of the verbal code.

    d. Each type of memory is based on similar, abstract, propositional coding schemas.

34. The most direct experimental evidence on the question of whether images are stored in memory comes from studies on:
    (a). Page 142-143. Factual.

    a. making images of hidden objects

    b. concrete and abstract words

    c. studies on mnemonic techniques

    d. memory of imaged words

35. The ability to discriminate between memory for perceived events and memory for thought is known as:
    (b). Page 146. Factual.

    a. discrimination task

    b. reality monitoring

    c. sensory-thought phenomena

    d. synthesia

TRUE -FALSE

1. The generation effect could serve as evidence to validate the levels of processing hypothesis.

   (true).

2. The inability to generate an answer for a word fragment will still allow you to remember that word better in a memory test than a word that is merely read.

   (true).

3. Memory for a sentence, such as "is a cat an animal, " is better than for a sentence such as "is a stone an animal?" due to the congruity effect.

   (true).

4. Self-generated memory cues are remembered less well than material generated by computer.

   (false).

5. Abstract words are remembered just as well as concrete words.

   (false).

6. The distinctiveness hypothesis predicts that under some circumstances nonsemantic information can be just as well remembered as semantic information.

   (true).

7. A tip-of-the-tongue is a verbal retrieval problem only.

   (true).

8. Memory for word pairs is more likely to be confused if the words are related to each other and your task is to list the similarities between the words.

   (true).

9. Making a mental image of a list of unrelated words to aid your memory is known as a mnemonic technique.

   (true).

10. Eyewitness testimony is usually very good, and the memory cannot be modified.

    (false).

11. Distinctiveness and organization are both important to memory because one is looking at the similarity among events, while the other is looking at the differences among event.

    (true).

12. According to dual coding theory, we should have better memory for a list of words we read and then formed a mental image of, because we would have stored the two memories in two different places.

    (false).

13. A mnemonic technique is a neurophysiological method of tracing memory images.

   (false).

14. A person is more likely to remember material that has been rated for its pleasantness than material rated for its personal relevance.

   (false).

15. Organization in memory does not occur unless the material presented for memory forces an organizational process at encoding.

   (false).

ESSAY

1. Given an experiment where subjects are shown a list of words, such as *PROCESS, LABORATORY, or DATA,* half the subjects are given a semantic orienting task of rating the words for how pleasant they are, while the other half is asked to pronounce the words according to stressed syllable. Later, both groups are given a recall test. Explain levels of processing and the distinctiveness hypothesis and how each would predict performance. Which theory did the research support?

2. Organization is thought to be good for memory because it focuses on the similarities among to-be-remembered items, while distinctiveness is thought to be good for memory because it illustrates the differences in items. How do each of the theories support their claims, and which is better for memory and why?

3. In the generation effect, even material that was not generated but at least had effortful processing resulted in better memory than material that was just read. Explain this finding in the context of McDaniel, Wadill, and Einstein's theory that memory is a result of both relational and distinctive processing.

4. If you are given a list of words to study and you read them and then make an image of them, you are going to remember them better than someone who just memorized them. Explain these findings in the context of Paivio's theory of dual-coding.

5. How are organization and elaboration related?

CHAPTER 6
RETRIEVAL PROCESSES

A. KEY TERMS

cue	generation-recognition
associative strength	cue-dependent
encoding specificity	implicit memory
episodic memory	explicit memory
semantic memory	dissociation
procedural memory	perceptual identification
propositional memory	modality effect
context independent	processing account
retrieval	conceptually driven
single-process theory	data-driven
recognition memory	automatic processes
recall memory	control processes
frequency	repetition effect
decay theory	proactive interference
frequency	retroactive interference
response competition	state dependent effects

B.   DEMONSTRATIONS/STUDENT RESEARCH PROJECTS

1. ENCODING SPECIFICITY

Students typically find the principles of encoding specificity difficult to understand. A simple experiment will make this clearer. First, ask students to tell you the first association that comes into their mind when they hear the following words: BOY, LARGE, NIGHT, SALT, TABLE, OVER, MORE.   It is assumed that they will generate the usual associations of girl, small, day, pepper, chair, under, less. This is to illustrate that there is a strong association between the cue words and the target words.

Tell the students that you are going to give them a list of word pairs that they are to study for a memory test. Pass out Handout 6-1, or call the word pairs out and have the students write them down. Allow them 5 minutes of study time. At the end of 5 minutes, tell the students to remove their word lists and that you are going to give them a cued recall test. Inform them that some of the cues will be the first word of the word pairs, which are the weakly associated cues that they studied in the handout, and that some of the cues will be words they have not seen before but that are strongly associated with the target words. Have students number their answers, and if they do not know a target word, they are to leave the space blank.   Use Handout 6-2 to cue the students for the recall test. Allow 6 seconds between cues. At the end of the recall test, have students tally the number of words they recalled for strongly associated cues, # 1, 4, 6, 8, 10, 11, 13, 15, 17, and 19, and a separate tally for the number of weakly associated words recalled for # 2, 3, 5, 7, 9, 12, 14, 16, 18, and 20. Students should do much better on the weakly-associated cued. Ask them to explain why.

2. RETROACTIVE AND PROACTIVE INTERFERENCE

Tell students that you are going to give them a series of cued recall tests. For List 1 instruct them to write down the words as you call them out. Give the students about 5 seconds between word pairs. At the end of the list, have students put away the written list and get a clean sheet of paper. Instruct them that you will call out the first word as a cue, and they are to recall the target word that was paired with the word. When this is finished, you will call out the correct answers, and students will score their recall. List 1 is found on Handout 6-3.

After the first list, repeat the procedure for List 2 found on Handout 6-4. Again call out the correct target words and have students score their data. After this list, tell students that you are going to repeat the cues for List 1, and they are to recall the target word again. Score this as List 3.

Students should score best on List 1 the first time, while recall on List 2 will demonstrate proactive interference. Recall of List 1 the second time will demonstrate retroactive interference.

HANDOUT 6-1

ENCODING SPECIFICITY STUDY LIST

1. WORM   -   APPLE

2. ENOUGH   -   LESS

3. SUNSHINE   -   DAY

4. WOOD   -   HAMMER

5. SKIRT   -   GIRL

6. SOME   -   PART

7. SNEEZE   -   PEPPER

8. PLATE   -   TABLE

9. CLOUD   -   WHITE

10. BLADE   -   KNIFE

11. STAND   -   LEG

12. HIDDEN   -   UNDER

13. LEAD   -   PENCIL

14. FLEA   -   DOG

15. BUCKLE   -   SHOE

16. SLIDE   -   DOWN

17. MAIL   -   READ

18. MEDICINE -   NURSE

19. STRANGE   -   ODD

20. LITTLE   -   SMALL

HANDOUT 6-2

CUED RECALL LIST FOR ENCODING SPECIFICITY TEST

1. ORANGE   STRONG ASSOCIATE
2. ENOUGH   WEAK ASSOCIATE
3. SUNSHINE   WEAK ASSOCIATE
4. NAIL   STRONG ASSOCIATE
5. SKIRT   WEAK ASSOCIATE
6. WHOLE   STRONG ASSOCIATE
7. SNEEZE   WEAK ASSOCIATE
8. CHAIR   STRONG ASSOCIATE
9. CLOUD   WEAK ASSOCIATE
10. FORK   STRONG ASSOCIATE
11. ARM   STRONG ASSOCIATE
12. HIDDEN   WEAK ASSOCIATE
13. PAPER   STRONG ASSOCIATE
14. FLEA   WEAK ASSOCIATE
15. SOCK   STRONG ASSOCIATE
16. SLIDE   WEAK ASSOCIATE
17. WRITE   STRONG ASSOCIATE
18. MEDICINE   WEAK ASSOCIATE
19. EVEN   STRONG ASSOCIATE
20. LITTLE   WEAK ASSOCIATE

PROACTIVE AND RETROACTIVE INTERFERENCE

LIST 1

1. BIRD   -   KISS

2. ROOM   -   SHOE

3. HAND   -   AUTO

4. HOSE   -   WRAP

5. TIME   -   GEAR

6. BOOT   -   STAR

7. DEER   -   FARM

8. LEAP   -   BEER

9. WHIP   -   MATE

10. CAMP   -   BANK

11. YEAR   -   LAMP

12. FEET   -   PUMP

13. NOTE   -   MINE

14. PEAR   -   WINE

15. VASE   -   SACK

16. BEAR   -   SEAT

17. TACK   -   LICE

18. OVEN   -   STEP

19. BEET   -   PLOT

20. MOLD   -   ROCK

HANDOUT 6-4

PROACTIVE AND RETROACTIVE INTERFERENCE

LIST 2

1. BIRD   -   LACE

2. ROOM   -   ROOT

3. HAND   -   REAR

4. HOSE   -   PACE

5. TIME   -   LEAF

6. BOOT   -   BACK

7. DEER   -   TOOL

8. LEAP   -   RACE

9. WHIP   -   TRAP

10. CAMP   -   CENT

11. YEAR   -   BULB

12. FEET   -   TRAY

13. NOTE   -   MANE

14. PEAR   -   BALL

15. VASE   -   DOLL

16. BEAR   -   HEAT

17. TACK   -   DOOR

18. OVEN   -   SAFE

19. BEET   -   NUMB

20. MOLD   -   VICE

C. ADDITIONAL RESOURCES

1. Suggested Readings

Bower, G. H. (1981). Mood and memory. *American Psychologist, 36,* 129-48.

Bower, G. H. (1987). Commentary on mood and memory. *Behavior and Research and Therapy, 25,* 443-45.

Einstein, G. O., & Hunt, R. R. (1980). Levels of processing and organization: Additive effects of individual item and relational processing. *Journal of Experimental Psychology: Human Learning and Memory, 6,* 588-98.

Graf, P., Mandler, G., & Haden, M. (1982). Simulating amnesic symptoms in normal subjects. *Science, 218,* 1243-44.

Graf, P., & Ryan, L. (1990). Transfer-appropriate processing for implicit and explicit memory. *Journal of Experimental Psychology: Learning, Memory and Cognition, 16,* 634-47.

Hirshman, E., Snodgrass, J. G., Mindes, J., & Feenan, K. (1990). Conceptual priming in fragment completion. *Journal of Experimental Psychology: Learning, Memory and Cognition, 16,* 634-47.

Hunt, R. R., Elliot, J. M. (1980). The role of nonsemantic information in memory: Orthographic distinctiveness effects upon retention. *Journal of Experimental Psychology: General, 109,* 49-74.

Mantyla, T., & Nilsson, L. (1983). Are my cues better than your cues? *Scandinavian Journal of Psychology, 24,* 303-12.

Mantyla, T., & Nilsson, L. (1988). Cue distinctiveness and forgetting: Effectiveness of self-generated retrieval cues in delayed recall. *Journal of Experimental Psychology: Learning, Memory, and Cognition, 14,* 502-09.

Mantyla, T. (1986). Optimizing cue effectiveness: Recall of 500 and 600 incidentally learned words. *Journal of Experimental Psychology: Learning, Memory, and Cognition, 1,* 66-71.

Nelson, T. D., Gerler, D., & Narens, L. (1984). Accuracy of feeling-of-knowing judgments for predicting perceptual identification and relearning. *Journal of Experimental Psychology: General, 113,* 282-300.

Nelson, D., & Borden, R. C. (1977). Encoding and retrieval effects of dual sensory-semantic cues. *Memory and Cognition, 5,* 457-61.

Roediger, H., & Blaxton, T. A. (1987). Retrieval modes produce dissociations in memory for surface information. *Memory and learning.* Hillsdale, NJ: Lawrence Erlbaum Associates, Publishers.

Roediger, H. L. III, & Blaxton, T. A. (1987). Effects of varying modality, surface features, and retention interval on priming in word-fragment completion. *Memory and Cognition, 15,* 379-88.

Roediger, H. L. III, & Blaxton, T. A., & Challis, B. H. (1990). Explaining dissociations between implicit and explicit measures of retention: A processing account. In H. L. Roediger & F. I. M. Craik (Eds.) *Varieties of memory and consciousness: Essays in honour of Endel Tulving.* Hillsdale, NJ: Lawrence Erlbaum Associates.

Tulving, E., & Thompson, D. M. (1973). Encoding specificity and retrieval processes in episodic memory. *Psychological Review, 82,* 261-71.

Watkins, O. C., & Watkins, M. J. (1975). Buildup of proactive inhibition as a cue-overload effect. *Journal of Experimental Psychology: Learning, Memory, and Cognition, 1,* 442-52.

2. Videotapes

Human memory, (1980). Harcourt Brace Jovanovich, 1250 Sixth Avenue, San Diego, CA 92101
The study of memory. Films for the Humanities and Sciences.

D. CHAPTER 6   TEST ITEMS

MULTIPLE-CHOICE

1. You are studying for a cued recall test and for the to-be-remembered words, you are given both strongly associated cues and weakly associated cues. At the test session you will be cued with both strong and weak cues, some of which you had at the study session and some of which you did not have at the study session. The following matrix represents the experiment.

TEST CUES		
	WEAK	STRONG
WEAK	Cell 1	Cell 2
STRONG	Cell 3	Cell 4

According to the associative strength model, which of the four cells would score the highest memory performance?
    (a). Page 154. Conceptual.

a. either cell 2 or 4, because it would not matter if the cues were present at input as long as the strongly associated cues are present at test

b. either cell 3 or 4, because strongly associated cues are necessary at the test session only, and encoding cues are unimportant

c. either cell 1 or 4, because as long as you are tested with the same cues that you encoded at study, you will be able to retrieve the event

d. cell 4 only, because the strongly associated cues are encoded at study and must match at test in order to trigger memory

2. For the following matrix, according to the encoding specificity model which of the four cells would score the highest memory performance?
    (c). Page 156. Conceptual.

TEST CUES		
	WEAK	STRONG
WEAK	Cell 1	Cell 2
STRONG	Cell 3	Cell 4

a. either cell 2 or 4, because it would not matter if the cues were present at input as long as the strongly associated cues are present at test

b. either cell 3 or 4, strongly associated cues are necessary at the test session only, encoding cues are unimportant

c. either cell 1 or 4, as long as you are tested with the same cues encoded at study, you will be able to retrieve the event

d. cell 4 only, strongly associated cues are encoded at study and must match at test to trigger memory

3. In the associative strength theory, when one word is cued in memory, there is a spread of this activation to other related cues. This predicts that the strength of an association between one word and a second activated word is a function of:
   (b). Page 155. Conceptual.

   a. organizational relatedness

   b. semantic distance

   c. economy of storage

   d. categorical storage

4. That the word *GREEN* might serve as an effective cue for remembering the word GRASS involves which of the following theories of cue effectiveness?
   (a). Page 154. Conceptual.

   a. associative strength

   b. associative weakness

   c. encoding specificity

   d. encoding generality

5. The phenomena of encoding specificity refers to a relation between which of the following?
   (d). Page 156-157. Conceptual.

   a. percent of recognition and the percent of recall

   b. the encoding condition and percent of recall

   c. the level of encoding and depth of processing

   d. the encoding condition and the retrieval condition

6. The principle of encoding specificity states that:
   (a). Page 156. Factual.

   a. the probability of retrieval is better if the context or cue at test time matches the context or cue when the information was encoded

   b. the probability of retrieval of correct retrieval is independent of inference processes

   c. retrieval is improved if the context at test time is different than the context at encoding time

   d. retrieval errors are based on structural changes that occur during storage, rather than during encoding

7. Which of the following are the two major theories of cue effectiveness?
   (c). Page 154-156. Factual.

   a. levels of processing, associative strength

   b. imagery, cue effectiveness

   c. associative strength, encoding specificity

   d. encoding specificity, levels of processing

8. According to associative strength model, if the word *PET* is activated in memory then other related words, such as *DOG,* will also be activated. This is known as:
   (d). Page 154. Conceptual.

   a. cue effectiveness

   b. trickle-down theory

   c. retrieval probability

   d. spreading activation

9. The transfer of information from long-term memory to short-term memory or from a latent state to a state of consciousness is known as:
   (a). Page. 158. Conceptual.

   a. episodic

   b. semantic

   c. procedural

   d. propositional

10. A theory that predicts that an effective retrieval cue is one which was present when the to-be-remembered event occurred is called:
    (b). Page 156-157. Factual.

    a. associative strength

    b. encoding specificity

    c. associative network model

    d. state dependent model

11. If you can remember the name of your first grade teacher, you are using _____ memory.
    (a). Page 158. Conceptual.

    a. episodic

    b. semantic

    c. procedural

    d. propositional

12. Encoding specificity is said to apply only to _____ memory.
    (c). Page 166. Conceptual.

    a. semantic

    b. procedural

    c. episodic

    d. dissociative

13. A theory that predicts that an effective retrieval cue is one which was present when the to-be-remembered event occurred is called:
    (b). Page. 166. Factual.

    a. associative strength

    b. encoding specificity

    c. associative network model

    d. state dependent model

14. Amnesic patients perform well on fragment completion tests of word lists but perform poorly on recall tests. This normal performance on implicit tests of memory is strong evidence for:
    (a). Page 166. Conceptual.

    a. separate memory systems

    b. inadequate testing procedures for persons with memory deficits

    c. an argument that implicit and explicit memory are related procedures

    d. semantic and episodic memory systems

15. Procedural memory is most likely to:
    (d). Page 160. Conceptual.

    a. be context independent

    b. govern your general skills, such as walking

    c. be automatic and unconscious

    d. all of the above

16. The primary difference between recall and recognition memory is that:
    (d). Page 163. Conceptual.

    a. recognition memory only requires a decision that the item has already been seen

    b. recall memory requires a generation phase and then a recognition decision process

    c. recognition memory is better because it has the best possible cue which is the old item itself

    d. all of the above

17. Encoding specificity is most compatible with:
    (c). Page 161. Conceptual.

    a. cue-dependent forgetting

    b. interference theory

    c. two-process theory

    d. decay theory

18. Tulvings's proposal of HERA (Hemispheric Encoding/Retrieval Asymmetry) model of memory proposes that:
    (b). Page 160. Factual.

    a. if a stimulus is seen or heard on one side of the brain, i.e., the left, that the right side of the brain will encode that information but that the memory will be stored in the left side of the brain.

    b. encoding has been found to predominantly activate the left prefrontal cortex, whereas episodic retrieval is strongly associated with activation in the right prefrontal cortex

    c. encoding and retrieval can occur on either the right or left side of the brain, and the process is not always consistent

    d. all of the above

19. Tulving's proposal that the episodic and semantic memory systems are distinct and separate systems is known as:
    (a). Page 160. Factual.

    a. HESA (Hemispheric Episodic/Semantic Asymmetry)

    b. encoding specificity

    c. brain ES

    d. study-test congruency

20. Dave is an amnesic patient who is given a list of words to study. He is later given a recall test of the list and is unable to recall any of the words. Later, Dave is given the same list of words but with only the first three letters of each word filled in and he is asked to finish completing the word. Dave now performs as well as a nonamnesic patient. This suggests that:
    (b). Page 165-170. Conceptual.

    a. his conscious memory is intact, but there is a problem with verbal retrieval

    b. his implicit memory system is normal, but his explicit memory system is dysfunctional

    c. both his recall and recognition retrieval processes are operating at an explicit level

    d. his propositional memory is dysfunctional, but his procedural memory is normal

21. The generation effect does not occur when using implicit memory tests. This suggests that:
    (a). Page 165. Conceptual.

    a. effortful processing is specific to explicit memory tests

    b. implicit memory tests do not require the retrieval of sensory information

    c. that verbal recall is restricted by explicit memory tests

    d. recall or recognition are tasks that are inappropriate to tests of explicit memory

22. The differences between implicit and explicit memory tests include all of the following except:
    (d). Page 165-170. Factual.

    a. explicit tests are context dependent, but implicit tests are context independent

    b. the cues required for implicit and explicit tests are different

    c. explicit tests instruct people to intentionally remember, while implicit tests have no intentional memory requirements

    d. both implicit and explicit memory tests are activating the same cognitive processes of memory

23. In testing _____, episodic memory is the type of memory tested.
    (d). Page 166. Factual.

    a. stem-completion

    b. perceptual-identification

    c. word association

    d. recall

24. If a list of study words is read to you and you are later given a visual fragment-completion test of those words, you are not going to do as well on the test as the person who was presented the words in the same sensory modality at both study and test. This is known as:
    (a). Page 167. Factual.

    a. modality effect

    b. conceptually driven processing

    c. semantic network effect

    d. sensory congruity effect

25. The processing account of memory predicts that if the same mental processes are used in both a prior study experience and the subsequent test:
    (c). Page 167. Conceptual.

    a. proactive interference will occur

    b. dissociations will occur

    c. performance on the test will be improved

    d. retrieval will be faster

26. Which of the following would be the best test of conceptually driven processing?
    (c). Page 168. Conceptual

    a. Fill in the following fragment: LIGHT - R_GH_.

    b. Complete the stem: ANIMAL- D__.

    c. Who was the first president of the United States?

    d. How many vowels are in the following word: BOOK.?

94

27. If you are given the word pair *BUSHEL - BASHFUL* at a study session, and later shown the cue *BUSHEL- B_SH_U_* to fill in the second word, this would be considered:
   (d). Page 168. Factual.

   a. data-driven processing

   b. graphemic cued recall

   c. episodic memory

   d. all of the above

28. Prior processing of some event will subsequently facilitate later processing of the same event. This is known as:
   (a). Page 172. Factual.

   a. repetition effect

   b. cue dependent remembering

   c. conceptually driven processing

   d. proactive learning

29. When new learning disrupts memory for material that was previously learned, it is called _____ interference.
   (d). Page 176. Factual.

   a. state dependent

   b. proactive

   c. sequential

   d. retroactive

30. In an experiment, two groups of subjects are each given the same list of words to learn. After the study phase, the experimental group is given another list of similar words to learn also, while the control group listens to music. Both groups are then tested for the recall of the words from the first list. The results are most likely to be:
   (a). Page 176. Conceptual.

   a. the experimental group will do worse that the control group because of retroactive interference

   b. the experimental group will do worse than the control   group because proactive interference will occur

   c. the experimental group will do better than the control group because proactive interference will occur in the   control

   d. the control group will do worse because retroactive interference will occur in the control group.

31. The reasons that we cannot retrieve something from the memory system is because of all of the following EXCEPT:
    (b). Page 177. Factual.

    a. response competition

    b. cue dependent effects

    c. ineffective cues

    d. all of the above are reasons for retrieval failure

32. Tulving has demonstrated that retroactive interference can be reduced when their are more specific retrieval cues for memory. He therefore proposes that instead of unlearning or response competition as explanations for forgetting, that _____ is a better explanation.
    (a). Page 179. Factual.

    a. cue-dependent forgetting

    b. proactive interference

    c. verbal retrieval failure

    d. context independent forgetting

33. If you are in class and need to remember the material for a test, all of the following EXCEPT _____ will increase your ability to remember.
    (c). Page. 171. Factual.

    a. elaboration of the lecture material to other known facts

    b. concentrating and paying attention to the lecture

    c. taking meticulous notes but not studying them again till test time

    d. organizing the lecture into topics from the book or previous lecture

34. If you were in a angry mood when you studied for this test, you are more likely to do best on this test if your mood is now due to study-test congruency:
    (c). Page 167. Conceptual.

    a. happy

    b. sad

    c. angry

    d. calm

35. Tulving and Psotka suggest that retroactive interference occurs because:
    (a). Page 179. Factual.

    a. the interfering material results in failure to access the stored information

    b. two episodic memories interfere with the semantic memory needed to answer the question

    c. there is decay of the first list

    d. all of the above could be appropriate answers

TRUE FALSE

1. Encoding specificity does not apply to semantic memory.

    (true).

2. It is always the case that a strongly associated cue leads to better memory than does a weakly associated cue.

    (false).

3. Procedural memory is the psychological processes that are involved in skill performance.

    (true).

4. In encoding specificity, you will have better memory for a word if you have the same cue at encoding as you do at retrieval.

    (true).

5. Personal, autobiographical memory is episodic memory.

    (true).

6. Encoding specificity proposes a generate-recognition theory of retrieval.

    (false).

7. The generate-recognition theory of memory proposes that recall and recognition have the same retrieval demands.

    (false).

8. A recall test is a test of implicit memory.

    (false).

9. If a student generates highly distinctive cues for a list of 600 words, and these cues are later used as retrieval cues for these words, these students have a correct retrieval rate of 90%.

    (true).

10. An amnesic patient can be given a list of words to remember and on memory tests can score 0% on a recall test, but close to 100% on a fragment-completion test.

    (true).

11. Semantic memory is context dependent.

    (false).

12. The modality effect is when the encoded sensory mode is the only way that a person can recall the information.

    (false).

13. Data-driven processing is processing that is guided by the physical features of the presented information.

    (true).

14. State dependent effects are a phenomenon where memory for verbally declared information is better than for auditory information.

(false).

15. Control processes are consciously monitored processes which have the purposeful intent to remember something.

(true).

ESSAY

1. A group of amnesic patient are given a list of 20 words to study for a recall test. They are later tested for their memory. Half of the patients are given a recall test, and the other half are given a word fragment-completion test. The patients with the recall test did very poorly, while the fragment completion patients had a high performance. Are these findings consistent with the processing account of data-driven and conceptually driven processing? Why or why not?

2. Tulving performed an experiment in which he gave subjects word pairs to study, such as *GLUE-CHAIR*, and then cued with the first word, subjects were able to recall the second word. He later gave the subjects a recognition test of the target second word after pairing them with a new cue word, *TABLE-CHAIR*. He found that there was a high percentage of recognition failure of previously recalled words. Explain this in terms of one-process and generate-recognize theories.

3. Given a list of words, one group is given a semantic orienting task by being asked to make a sentence with each of the words. The control group is asked to count the number of vowels, a nonsemantic orienting task. Later, half of each group is tested for recall and half are tested for a fragment completion test. How does each group perform on the different tests? Explain this in the context of a processing account of memory.

4. How could distinctive retrieval cues counteract proactive or retroactive interference?

CHAPTER 7

THE STRUCTURE AND FUNCTION AND KNOWLEDGE

A. KEY TERMS

expert performance
associative network model
propositional network
typically effect
characteristic features
perceptual categories
hierarchical organization
cognitive economy
semantic distance effect
teachable language comprehender

spreading activation
feature set theory
defining features
prototypes
attribute models
category size effect
superordinate
exemplar theory
abstract knowledge

B. DEMONSTRATION/STUDENT ACTIVITIES

1. VERIFICATION OF TYPICALITY

In this experiment, you are going to demonstrate that members of a category that are more typical are identified faster than atypical members of a category. You can either test one student at a time with a stopwatch, or if you have an instrument that tests reaction time, you may test as many students simultaneously as you wish. Handout 7-1 has lists of category and member items for you to call out.

Tell the students that you will call out the category topic first, and then you will give them 10 items. Tell them that some of these items will be members of that category, and some will not be related. Ask them to simply decide whether or not the item belongs in the category by answering yes or no to each item.

All items are actually members of the category, but some are typical and some are not The atypical members of each category are marked on the list with an asterisk. The reaction time for each item is recorded. Scoring is done by calculating a mean for the items which are members of the category and a mean for the items which are atypical members of the category. Results should show that there is a faster reaction time for typical category members than items which are not typical members of the category.

2. SPREADING ACTIVATION.

In Handout 7-2, there are three lists of words. Give students one list at a time and measure their reaction time for completing each of the lists. The task for the student is to look at each string of letters and decide whether or not it is a real word. Students are to check the strings that are real words and place an X on the strings that are not real words.

The first list includes some words which are weakly associated with the following word. The second list includes no associated word. List 3 includes words which are strongly associated with the following words. List 4 includes word pairs that are in the same category. Students should perform best on the third and fourth lists, followed by the first list and, finally, the second list.

If you have several students participating, you might distribute the order of the lists differently to each student to prevent a practice effect. However, this effect is so slight that it is not absolutely necessary to do this.

Besides a reaction time for each of the lists, score the data by calling out which are real words and which are not for each list. This is important to do, because students make a lot of mistakes doing this test. Count the number of errors per each list. Discuss these findings in terms of spreading activation and priming effects.

HANDOUT 7-1

VERIFICATION OF TYPICALITY EFFECT

CATEGORY I

ANIMAL

1. ELEPHANT
2. HORSE
3. HIPPOPOTAMUS*
4. GOAT
5. AARDVARK*
6. CHINCHILLA*
7. RABBIT
8. COYOTE*
9. MOUSE
10. LEMMING*

CATEGORY 2

COLORS
1. YELLOW
2. TAUPE*
3. FUSHIA*
4. PURPLE
5 . MAUVE*
6. TURQUOISE
7. PRIMROSE*
8. BROWN
9. WHITE
10. MAROON*

CATEGORY 3

TOOL
1. HACKSAW
2. PENKNIFE*
3. GRINDSTONE*
4. CROWBAR
5. HAMMER
6. TROWEL*
7 SCREWDRIVER
8. BEVEL*
9. CHAINSAW
10. CHISEL *

CATEGORY 4

FRUIT

1. BANANA
2. CANTALOUPE
3. PERSIMMON*
4. KIWI*
5. WATERMELON
6. PAPAYA*
7. STRAWBERRY
8. ORANGE
9. BOYSENBERRY*
10. FIG*

CATEGORY 5

CLOTHING
1. BLOUSE
2. KNICKERS*
3. SHORTS
4. PETTICOAT*
5. SUIT
6. PONCHO*
7. OVERCOAT
8. PINAFORE*
9. CARDIGAN*
10. JACKET

HANDOUT 7-2

SPREADING ACTIVATION WORD LISTS

LIST 1		LIST 2		LIST 3		LIST 4	
BOOK	____	FARM	____	PEPPER	____	ROSE	____
PAGE	____	JEWEL	____	SALT	____	DAISY	____
TUME	____	GACE	____	HERT	____	GREEF	____
BULE	____	HASAL	____	INCET	____	SORRER	____
RULER	____	DESIGN	____	DOCTOR	____	OREGANO	____
LINE	____	FERDER	____	NURSE	____	GARLIC	____
CHACK	____	TOOR	____	TABLE	____	COFFEE	____
JULE	____	SAND	____	CHAIR	____	JUICE	____
RADIO	____	HURCH	____	BLANT	____	FERER	____
MUSIC	____	FLOOR	____	TREAL	____	SACER	____
BLISH	____	COMET	____	QUEEN	____	WAGON	____
OUT	____	RAKE	____	KING	____	SCOOTER	____
EXIT	____	NOZZLE	____	WALK	____	EMERALD	____
TOLLE	____	PADE	____	RUN	____	RUBY	____
BOTTLE	____	RADAR	____	KEELE	____	LESAR	____
JAR	____	SCREEN	____	PLETE	____	GRASER	____
GLOBE	____	MILDEW	____	LARER	____	BACER	____
WORLD	____	SPRAG	____	NETTE	____	SIBER	____
SCEAR	____	LIMET	____	CUP	____	MAPLE	____
BLEER	____	REFAGE	____	SAUCER	____	PINE	____
PAINT	____	PORCH	____	GRAFE	____	UBER	____
COLOR	____	SAMPLE	____	KNIFE	____	HUNER	____
SHELL	____	LOBER	____	FORK	____	MILE	____
FISH	____	BLUSH	____	SUN	____	INCH	____
FATTEL	____	RASER	____	MOON	____	SHIRT	____
BACE	____	LETTLE	____	HANGLE	____	PANTS	____
LACE	____	YARD	____	LABE	____	HABER	____
RIBBON	____	SYRINGE	____	BLANTE	____	APPLE	____
BINES	____	FLUTE	____	TRICH	____	BANANA	____
PLASTER	____	STYLE	____	WALK	____	COMET	____
MOLD	____	VIOLET	____	RUN	____	PLANET	____
MOAD	____	YIELD	____	SATTLE	____	DANSER	____

C. ADDITIONAL RESOURCES

1. Suggested Readings

Anderson, J. R. (1974). Verbatim and propositional representational of sentences in immediate and long-term memory. *Journal of Verbal Learning and Verbal Behavior, 13*, 149-62.

Anderson, J. R. (1976). *Language, memory and thought.* Hillsdale, NJ: Erlbaum.

Eylon, B., & Rief, F. (1984). Effects of knowledge organization on task performance. *Cognition and Instruction, 1*, 5-44.

Loftus, E. (1974). Activation of semantic memory. *American Journal of Psychology, 86*, 331-37.

Meyer, D. E., & Schvaneveldt, R.W. (1971). Facilitation in recognizing pairs of words: Evidence of a dependence between retrieval operations. *Journal of Experimental Psychology, 90*, 227-34.

Rips, L. J., Shobin, E. J. & Smith, E. E., (1973). Semantic distance and the verification of semantic relations. *Journal of Verbal Learning and Verbal Behavior, 12*, 1-20.

D. CHAPTER 7   TEST ITEMS

MULTIPLE-CHOICE

1. According to Ellis and Hunt, high knowledge individuals are those who:
   (a). Page 184. Factual.

   a. have highly developed skills in a particular area

   b. are very high in general intelligence

   c. have a higher than average IQ

   d. score very high on memory tests of general knowledge

2. In research on expert performance, Group one consisted of subjects who have a high-knowledge of baseball (HK group), and Group two with low-knowledge (LK) of baseball. Both groups were read a passage which described a game at the end of the first inning. The results showed that:
   (b). Page 184. Factual.

   a. LK subjects remembered more because their lack of knowledge decreased retroactive interference

   b. HK remembered more detailed and relevant information

   c. LK reported more relevant details because they could not tell the difference between relevant and irrelevant information

   d. surprisingly, LK were far superior in their ability to predict what was likely to happen next in so much that the researchers attributed to "beginner's luck"

3. According to Ellis and Hunt, results from studies by Voss and colleagues using high-knowledge and low-knowledge subjects and a fictitious baseball game suggest that:
   (a). Page 184. Factual.

   a. knowledge provides a framework for interpreting and organizing material

   b. knowledge disrupts organization and impairs memory

   c. the meaning of specific events is not related to semantic memory

   d. our interpretation of new experiences is independent of our knowledge base

4. The primary goal of research concerning semantic memory has been to describe the _____ of knowledge.
   (a). Page. 185. Factual.

   a. structure

   b. function

   c. purpose

   d. use

5. According to the TLC associative network model, which of the following statements would take the longest time to verify as true?
      (d). Page 187. Factual.

   a. Is a a robin a bird?

   b. Is a penguin a bird?

   c. Is a bird an animal?

   d. Is a robin an animal?

   e. Is a mammal an animal?

6. Cognitive economy refers to:
      (b). Page 187. Factual.

   a. the system's ability to make the fastest possible search for retrieval of to-be-remembered material

   b. the characteristics of any concept are stored at the highest hierarchical node, and there is no redundancy in the system

   c. in activation of a node, the adjoining nodes are activated at the same time, resulting in the most efficient retrieval with the least processing resources used

   d. the thriftiness of the long-term memory system in storage and retrieval of information

7. The two assumptions of associative network model are:
      (b). Page 187. Factual.

   a. node activation, storage economy

   b. cognitive economy, hierarchical organization

   c. spreading activation, cue effectiveness

   d. encoding specificity, associative strength

8. On a reaction time test, which of the following would take the least time to react to according to the TLC associative network model?
      (d). Page 187. Factual.

   a. A canary has skin.

   b. A canary is an animal.

   c. A canary can fly.

   d. A canary is a canary.

9. If you were asked, "Does a canary have skin?" or "Is a canary a canary?" you would take less time to answer the second statement. The reason that it would take less reaction time to verify one statement over another is:
    (c). Page 187-188. Factual.

    a. conceptual knowledge seems to be organized in a hierarchical way

    b. features or characteristics that are directly relevant to certain nodes (canary node) are stored with those nodes in the network structure

    c. people require slightly more time to access information that is presumed to be farther from the starting point in the network structure

    d. all of the above

10. Collins and Quillian in their associate network model demonstrated that:
    (d). Page 188. Factual.

    a. conceptual knowledge seems to be organized in a hierarchical way

    b. features or characteristics that are directly relevant to certain nodes (canary node) are stored with those nodes in the network structure

    c. people require slightly more time to access information that is presumed to be farther from the starting point in the network structure

    d. all of the above

11. In TLC, the principle that larger categories require more time for a mental search than do smaller categories is known as:
    (c). Page 197. Factual.

    a. typicality effect

    b. spreading activation

    c. category size effect

    d. cognitive economy

12. In an experiment of sentence verification time, Conrad asked, "An apple is edible" or "An apple has seeds." According to TLC, the word *edible* should be stored with the hierarchical node of *food*, but *seeds* should be stored with apple. Therefore, it should take longer to verify the first sentence. Conrad found no differences in reaction time for the two sentences and concluded that instead of hierarchical storage:
    (a). Page 198. Factual.

    a. episodic memory places items into semantic memory according to the sequence in which they occurred

    b. semantic memory predicts that speed of retrieval of a memory is predicted by the temporal encoding of the event

    c. some subordinates are more semantically related to the superordinate node than others and require less verification time

    d. it takes longer to trace an episodic memory than a semantic memory

13. The member *OSTRICH* is less typical of the category *BIRD* than is the member *ROBIN*. According to the semantic distance effect, it would:
    (b). Page 197. Conceptual.

    a. take more time to verify that a *ROBIN* is a bird

    b. take more time to verify that *OSTRICH* is a bird

    c. take equal time to verify that a ROBIN and an OSTRICH are birds because they both are semantically related

    d. take less time to verify that an *OSTRICH* is bird

14. The semantic distance effects states that:
    (c). Page 198. Factual.

    a. episodic memory places items into semantic memory according to the sequence in which they occurred

    b. semantic memory predicts that speed of retrieval of a memory is predicted by the temporal encoding of the event

    c. some subordinates are more semantically related to the superordinate node than others and require less verification time

    d. it takes longer to trace an episodic memory than a semantic memory

15. The typicality effect is demonstrating the concept of:
    (c). Page 198. Conceptual.

    a. neural reaction time

    b. hierarchical nodes

    c. semantic distance

    d. economy of storage

16. According to Smith, Shoben, and Rip's feature model, "a robin is a bird" is verified faster than "a robin is an animal" because there is:
    (a). Page 198. Conceptual.

    a. a greater overlap of features

    b. a greater activation of just characteristic features

    c. more length of associations

    d. more complexity of propositions

17. It takes longer to verify the question, "Is a DOG an mammal?" than it does to verify the question "Is a DOG an animal?" This result poses problems for the associative network models of memory because:
> (a). Page 210. Conceptual.

a. it should take longer to search the larger category of animal

b. *DOG* is more semantically related to mammal than to animal

c. once *DOG* is activated, the spread of activation should be immediate to the superordinate of mammal

d. *DOG* is a more typical exemplar of animal than mammal

18. _____ features are central to the meaning of a concept, while _____ features are particular, but not necessary to the concept.
> (b). Page 211. Factual.

a. associative; semantic

b. defining; characteristic

c. semantic; episodic

d. characteristic; defining

19. One feature of birds is flying. According to the feature set theory, this is a _____ feature.
> (c). Page 211. Factual.

a. defining

b. hierarchical

c. characteristic

d. both a and c

20. According to the feature set theory, if asked "Is a robin a bird?", all features of both concepts are activated. The decision process of answering the question consists of:
> (d). Page 197. Factual.

a. activation of one node and the spread of activation to the second node

b. the ability to trace the path from the node of *ROBIN* to the node of *BIRD*

c. measuring the degree of activation of the two nodes

d. activation of both defining and characteristic features and a large overlap of features answering, "Yes"

21. According to the feature set theory, if asked, "Is an ostrich a bird?", there are only an intermediate number of overlapping features. The decision process must then complete a second phase which consists of:
    (c). Page 197. Factual.

    a. counting the overlap of defining and characteristic features of both concepts

    b. matching only the characteristic features

    c. matching only the defining features

    d. repeating the question and relying on other relevant semantic information

22. The primary way that the feature model represents a semantic relationship between two items is:
    (b). Page 198. Factual.

    a. the distance between the two nodes

    b. the number of overlapping features that are activated

    c. the degree of activation spread from one representation to another

    d. the number of hierarchical levels from one representational node to another

23. The differences between the associative network model and the feature set theory is that for the former semantic relationships between concepts are expressed in terms of _____, while for the latter they are represented by _____.
    (a). Page 197. Factual.

    a. distance; number of overlapping features

    b. relatedness; semantic set size

    c. properties of features; activation

    d. typicality of belongingness; semantic distance

24. According to the propositional network theories, a proposition is:
    (b). Page 193. Factual.

    a. something that is proposed to replace semantic knowledge

    b. the smallest unit of knowledge which can be asserted

    c. a connection between neural nodes which forms an agreement of semantic relatedness

    d. a thinking process which produces knowledge

25. According to the propositional network model, the sentence, "Sam sells vegetable to Guido," consists of _____ propositions.
    (d). Page 193. Factual.

    a. three

    b. five

    c. one

    d. four

26. A _____ is the best or most representative example of a category.
    (b). Page 199. Factual.

    a. relevant example

    b. prototype

    c. problem representation

    d. framing decision

27. The three theories of categorization are:
    (b). Page 196-209. Factual.

    a. associative network, encoding specificity, and switch model

    b. attribute, prototype, and exemplar

    c. feature set theory, focus gambling, and conjunction

    d. basic level, linguistic, and logical

28. A perceptual prototype would consist of:
    (c). Page 200. Factual.

    a. categories of visual perceptions

    b. frequencies of light or sound that are the brightest or loudest

    c. the best examples of particular colors; the best blue, the best green

    d. any sensory information

29. After a patient with associative visual agnosia copied pictures of several drawings they then:
    (a). Page 203. Factual.

    a. still misidentified the drawings

    b. could identify the drawings verbally

    c. could identify the drawings by using gestural depiction

    d. none of the above, they could not reproduce the drawings

30. The study of patients with associative visual agnosia is important because:
    (b). Page 202. Factual.

    a. left brain lateralization is more susceptible to brain damage

    b. it tells us about the neural organization of semantic knowledge

    c. episodic memory systems are more affected by any sensory damage

    d. it will help in studying dementia

31. Jacoby and Witherspoon primed subjects with words which were both low frequency and atypical spellings. For example, they were given words such as, *HARE* or *REED*, which were not as typical a spelling as *READ* or *HAIR*. Following this presentation, subjects were given a spelling test. Without the priming, the higher frequency spelling would typically be used, but their subjects used the spelling of the primed words. This experiment demonstrates that:
    (a). Page 208. Factual.

    a. knowledge acquired over past experience can be altered due to a single episode

    b. knowledge is contextual

    c. the exemplar theory may be valid in its claims of episodic knowledge

    d. all of the above

32. The exemplar theory proposes that:
    (d). Page 208-209. Factual.

    a. knowledge is abstract

    b. knowledge is a combination of all of our experiences abstracted into the best example of an event

    c. knowledge is not episodic

    d. all knowledge is episodic

33. Subjects are given a pair of words (*MUFFLER = MUFFLER*) and asked to determine if the two words are the same or different from each other. Some of these word pairs are preceded with a category topic (*CLOTHING*) which primes the subject for the upcoming words. When the word pairs are typical members of a category, subjects responded faster than when the pairs are atypical. These results indicate that:
    (d). Page 207-210. Factual.

    a. there are no fuzzy boundaries in natural concepts

    b. there is a best example stored in memory

    c. development is culturally bound

    d. knowledge will be determined by specific prior event rather than by abstract rules

34. Subjects are given a series of objects varying in size, position, shape, and color and are asked to classify them into categories. Later, they are given a set of new objects and are asked if these are new or the same as before. The more similar the objects were to the original forms, the more likely they were to be remembered as old. This experiment validated:
    (b). Page 208. Factual.

    a. prototype theory

    b. exemplar theory

    c. attribute theory

    d. natural concepts

35. If I tell you to think of a fish and you think of its characteristics, such as gills, fins, no air, etc., you are thinking of its _____ attributes.
    (a). Page 197. Conceptual.

a. defining

b. characteristic

c. prototypical

d. all of the above

TRUE FALSE

1. Attribute models and associative network models both assume that the similarity of meaning among concepts is represented by distance.

   (false).

2. The category size effect predicts that given the category ANIMAL or given the category DOG, it would take less time to mentally search the smaller category of DOG than it would to do a search for the larger category of ANIMAL.

   (true).

3. Spelling is a cognitive skill that is regulated by semantic memory.

   (true).

4. According to associate network theory, if asked "Does a canary have skin?" you are able to verify this statement by tracing the activation of *CANARY* to the higher node of *ANIMAL* where the property of skin is stored.

   (true).

5. If I have a better representation of how a game is played than you do, you are still likely to be able to win at the game due to beginners elaboration of the spatial memory.

   (false).

6. A prototype is an abstracted schema of all the commonalties among members of a category.

   (true).

7. All associative network models of semantic memory stress that the link between concepts is determined by associations between the concepts.

   (true).

8. Semantic distance is the length of time that it takes to form two associations of unrelated items.

   (false).

9. Typicality effect is when most people produce the same associated word to a cue.

   (false).

10. Recognition of pictures is a type of memory subject to decline over a longer retention interval.

    (true).

11. It is likely that in concept learning a person learns both prototypes and features of a concept.

    (true).

12. The exemplar theory states that the semantic memory system mirrors reality, and there is no episodic memory.

    (false).

13. The TLC assumes the existence of a hierarchical organization in memory.

    (true).

14. Feature set theory agrees with TLC that there is a spread of activation to the hierarchical node.

(false).

15. Kintsch and Glass demonstrated that the more propositions that are in a sentence, the more difficulty people have in remembering it.

(true).

ESSAY

1. If asked "Is an OSTRICH a bird?" it would take you more time to respond than if asked "Is a ROBIN a bird?" How is this typicality effect explained by the feature set model?

2. How does a patient with a condition called *Agnosia* illustrate how knowledge is represented in our memory systems?

3. Describe the differences and similarities between associative network models and feature set theory.

4. In an experiment of sentence verification time, Conrad stated , "AN APPLE IS EDIBLE" or "AN APPLE HAS SEEDS." According to associate network model, *EDIBLE* should be stored with the hierarchical node of *FOOD*, but *SEEDS* should be stored with *APPLE*. Conrad found that there was no difference in verification time between the two sentences. How does this present problems for the associative network model of semantic memory?

5. In an experiment by Medin and Scheaffer, subjects are given a series of objects varying on size, position, form, and color and asked to classify them into categories. Later, they are given a set of new objects and asked if these are new or the same as before. The more similar the objects were to the original forms, the more likely they were to be remembered as old. What are the differences and similarities between the prototype theory and the exemplar theory, and how does this experiment validate or discount both of the theories?

CHAPTER 8
COMPREHENSION AND KNOWLEDGE

A. KEY TERMS

gist

theme

integration

presuppositions

response bias

logical inference

pragmatic inferences

constructive processes

schemas

temporal organization

spatial organization

scene schemas

event schemas

selective attention

framework effects

guiding retrieval

output editing

SP+T

reconstructive memory

culture specific

verbatim memory

B. DEMONSTRATIONS/STUDENT ACTIVITIES

1. ENCODING EFFECTS OF VERBAL INSTRUCTION

This demonstration will illustrate the effects of verbal instruction or theme on memory for a written passage. Handout 8-1 contains a description of a automobile accident as told by the involved person. Pick two students, or two groups of students, to listen to the passage and tell them that they will later have a recall test on the material. Tell one group of students that they are to listen to the passage from the perspective of an attending physician taking care of the victim. The second group is to take the perspective of the policeman who is trying to decide whose fault the accident was. After reading the passage, ask them to write down as much of the passage as they can remember. They can write down idea units instead of verbatim recall; the important issue is whether they recall the same information or not. Generally, there is a great difference in recall due to the theme given to them that guided their encoding.

2. VERBATIM MEMORY

Have the students read the story in the text at the beginning of chapter 8 to themselves, and then close the book and get out a clean sheet of paper. Tell them you are going to test their memory for immediate events, and you will read them a series of sentences. All they have to do is determine if the sentence is new or old. Tell them to number their paper 1 to 10 and write their answer beside each number. The questions are found on Handout 8-2. Have students score their answers and write their name on the answer sheet. At the end of the demonstration, take up the answer sheets, and save them until the next class when you will test their memory again and compare the scores for immediate versus delayed retrieval.

After the first test, ask the students to also write their answers to the following questions.

Is this man

1. rich or poor
2. educated or uneducated
3. young or old
4. married or widowed
5. employed or unemployed
6. Albert Einstein, Samuel Clement, or William Faulkner

Asking students to tell you the answers to these last questions will also demonstrate how information is relevant to personal schemas.

HANDOUT 8-1

ENCODING EFFECTS OF VERBAL INSTRUCTIONS

VERBAL PASSAGE OF AUTOMOBILE ACCIDENT

I was driving down the road very slowly and I was very warm, so I slowed down and rolled down the window. I continued driving slowly when I thought I saw the stoplight turn yellow, but I must have been mistaken because it then turned green. I must have had a leg cramp or something because when I went to accelerate, instead, I slammed on the brakes. I looked in my rear view mirror and saw the truck behind me headed very fast toward me, but I was paralyzed. After what seemed like a very long time, but was actually only seconds, the truck plowed into me and pushed me into the middle of the intersection. The force of the impact caused me to hit my head on the steering wheel and made my neck pop. As soon as the car stopped spinning, a blue Buick came charging through the intersection and hit my car from the other side, causing me to again hit my head on the steering wheel, and blood started pouring out of the cut.

I couldn't see very well and could not get out of the car, not only because my arm felt like it was broken, but because I had a car at every door blocking the way. So, I just stayed there until the police came.

HANDOUT 8-2

RECOGNITION FOR NEW AND OLD SENTENCES FROM PROSE PASSAGE

1. He missed Mississippi, and even more, he missed many of the lost values and traditions of the Old South.

(old).

2. As he got older, he missed the old southern ways of his Mississippi plantation home.

(new).

3. He looked toward the old whitewashed house where he would spend the rest of his life alone.

(new).

4. His daughters and wife affectionately referred to him as Papa.

(new).

5. He turned the block toward his large white clapboard house where he would spend the rest of his days in essential solitude.

(old).

6. Papa, dressed in a rumpled white suit, took a early-morning walk through the small town in southern Mississippi.

(new).

7. The chill in the air revived memories of warm, early autumn evenings on the verandah with wife and children.

(old).

8. The town where he now lived was so fast-paced and different in comparison to the early days in the Deep South.

(new).

9. As October began to settle in the Shennandoah Valley, he increasingly found his thoughts turning to his beloved Mississippi and the old plantation.
(old).

10. Papa, as he was affectionately known to his close family, took his usual morning walk through the sleepy, southern town.

(old).

C. ADDITIONAL RESOURCES

1. Suggested Readings

Abelson, R. P. (1981). Psychological status of the script concept. *American Psychologist, 36,* 715-29.

Brewer, W. F., & Treyens, J.C. (1981). Role of schemata in memory for places. *Cognitive Psychology, 13,* 207-30.

Friedman, A. (1979). Framing pictures: The role of knowledge in automatized encoding and memory for gist. *Journal of Experimental Psychology: General, 108,* 316-55.

Mandler, J. M. (1984). *Stories, scripts, and scenes: Aspects of schema theory.* Hillsdale, NJ: Erlbaum.

Potts, G. R. (1972). Information-processing strategies used in the encoding of linear orderings. *Journal of Verbal Learning and Verbal Behavior, 11,* 727-40.

Spiro, R. J. (1977). Remembering information from text: The "state of schema" approach. In R. C. Anderson, R. J. Spiro, & W. E. Montague (Eds.), *Schooling and the acquisition of knowledge.* Hillsdale, NJ: Erlbaum.

2. Videotapes

Fidelity of report, Film, William Ray, Pennsylvania State University, Audiovisual Department, Special Services Building, University Park, PA, 16802.

Human memory. Harcourt Brace Jovanovich, 1250 Sixth Avenue, San Diego, CA, 92101.

The study of memory. Films for the Humanities and Sciences.

D. CHAPTER 8 TEST ITEMS

MULTIPLE-CHOICE

1. Memory is sometimes facilitated by all but which of the following:
   (a). Page 218-222. Factual.

   a. marbleization

   b. themes

   c. inferences

   d. comprehension

2. The process of extracting the general meaning of a communication and discarding details is called _____.
   (b). Page 222. Factual.

   a. inference

   b. comprehension

   c. memory

   d. integration

3. The _____ of a passage of prose is the most likely information to be remembered.
   (c). Page 226. Conceptual.

   a. length

   b. details

   c. theme

   d. logical inferences

4. In comprehension of a prose passage that you are reading, you will be most likely to _____ the real details of the paragraph.
   (b). Page 222. Factual.

   a. remember

   b. disregard

   c. define

   d. integrate

5. _____ in written text provide guidance which facilitates integration of information during comprehension but at the risk of distorting understanding and memory of the material.
    (a). Page 222. Factual.

    a. Themes

    b. Plots

    c. Characters

    d. Chapters

6. Bransford and Franks presented subjects with partial input sentences derived from a more complex sentence. In later recognition tests, different kinds of sentences were presented: old sentences, new sentences that could be derived from the gist of the complex idea, and noncase sentences which were different in meaning form the old sentences or idea. Results indicated that:
    (d). Page 224. Factual.

    a. subjects readily distinguish old from new sentences

    b. the smaller the idea unit, the more sure the subject was that it was old

    c. subjects reported the noncase sentences to be old ideas

    d. individual sentences are not maintained in memory, but the separate ideas expressed by the old sentences are integrated into a general idea which consists of the gist of the message

7. A theme guides memory of a written passage because it aids the reader in _____ memory of the event.
    (c). Page 218-219. Factual.

    a. inferring

    b. storing

    c. reconstructing

    d. sorting

8. Loftus illustrated that people's testimony can be influenced by the way sentences were phrased. This is called _____.
    (a). Page 220. Factual.

    a. a presupposition

    b. reconstructive memory

    c. inferencing

    d. comprehension

9. Loftus showed subjects an automobile accident and then tested their memory for the event. The results indicated:
   (c). Page 220. Factual.

   a. memory was not influenced by how the questions were phrased

   b. all subjects were accurate in their memory performance

   c. subjects gave different reports depending on different presuppositions conveyed by how the questions were phrased

   d. eyewitness testimony given in court should be considered highly reliable

10. Elizabeth Loftus showed subjects an automobile accident scene and asked them to estimate how fast the cars were going when they _____ each other. Which of the following verbs caused subjects to estimate the highest speeds.
    (a). Page 220-221. Factual.

    a. smashed

    b. bumped

    c. hit

    d. contacted

11. Results from Loftus and Palmer's experiments indicate that the subject's response could actually be:
    (d). Page 221 Factual.

    a. some subliminal encoding of information

    b. an alteration in memory for the event

    c. a response bias due to the wording of the question

    d. both b and c

12. The implications of the Loftus and Palmer experiment are that:
    (b). Page 221. Factual.

    a. subjects could actually forget the old event, but with questioning at the test session, gist memory returns and they report events consistent with their own personal schemas

    b. subjects could integrate an old memory with presuppositions required by the test questions to form a new memory representation

    c. can be very accurate if subjects are instructed to attend to certain variables at encoding

    d. automobile accidents are the poorest events to test eyewitness testimony

13. The _____ is knowledge that must be activated in order for the statement to be understood: the _____ is knowledge which is activated after understanding the statement has occurred.
   (d). Page 221-222. Factual.

   a. logical inference; presupposition

   b. pragmatic inference; logical presupposition

   c. inference; pragmatic presupposition

   d. presupposition; inference

14. A _____ inference is shown by an example such as, "Bill is taller than Sue, and Sue is taller than Harry. Is Harry taller than Bill?"
   (a). Page 222-223. Conceptual.

   a. logical

   b. pragmatic

   c. gist

   d. reconstructive

15. "The student's performance forced the professor to flunk her. This assertion demands the inference that the student failed the course. Such inferences are called _____ inferences.
   (b). Page 222-223. Conceptual.

   a. assertional

   b. logical

   c. presuppositional

   d. pragmatic

16. A _____ inference is demanded by the assertion while the _____ inference is a reasonable assumption based on world knowledge.
   (a). Page 224. Factual.

   a. logical; pragmatic

   b. realistic; probable

   c. pragmatic; logical

   d. assertive; passive

17. If I said, "I went out to dinner last night and had a great meal," you might infer that I ate in a restaurant. This is called a _____ inference.
   (c). Page 224. Conceptual.

   a. logical

   b. presuppositional

   c. pragmatic

   d. rational

18. Business firms spend billions of dollars every year advertising their products. If you watch television for 3 hours, you are likely to see 27 minutes of commercials. Research discussed in your book indicates that advertising:
    (c). Page 240. Factual.

    a. is blatantly dishonest

    b. is a waste of the product firm's money

    c. promotes faulty inferences by viewers

    d. should be more carefully monitored by parents

19. In an experiment, subjects were shown a Listerine commercial talking about colds which said, "During the cold-catching season, have him gargle with full-strength Listerine. Watch his diet, and sleep, and there's a good chance he'll have fewer colds this year." When later questioned, "Does gargling with Listerine prevent colds?" subjects:
    (b). Page 240. Factual.

    a. unanimously reported no, there was no benefit of gargling

    b. unanimously reported yes

    c. were split on their answers of both yes and no

    d. 80% reported yes, but 20% reported no

20. Early research in inferences was interpreted to indicate that inferences occurred during _____, whereas more recent work suggests that inferences also occur during _____.
    (d). Page 224. Factual.

    a. encoding; recoding

    b. storage; retrieval

    c. encoding; storage

    d. retrieval; encoding

21. When you are given a title to read along with a passage of written material, you are more likely to recall the material better than if you were not given the title of the passage until the recall test. This indicates that:
    (c). Page 215. Conceptual.

    a. titles are important for storage and retrieval processes

    b. titles guide reconstruction of the event

    c. titles provide information at encoding that help construct the memory event

    d. encoding specificity is relevant when titles are given at encoding or retrieval

22. Memory for conversation or prose is assumed to be different from memory for word lists in that:
    (a). Page 227. Factual.

    a. discourse memory shows effects, such as elaboration and addition of self-generated information

    b. memory for word lists lasts longer than discourse memory

    c. word lists are specific to episodic memory

    d. discourse memory is not remembered in a connected way but only in modular fashion

23. Memory for conversation or prose is assumed to be the same as memory for word lists in that:
    (c). Page 227. Factual.

    a. memory is verbatim for both

    b. it has been shown that memory is encoded, stored in the same place, and retrieved the same for both

    c. information for both types of information is actively transformed and retained in an abstract, semantic code

    d. both are coded with the same verbal or motor activation

24. Schemas are frequently organized:
    (a). Page 228. Factual.

    a. temporally or spatially

    b. episodically or semantically

    c. sequentially

    d. by images

25. A cognitive representation or framework that consists of organized information people have about various concepts, events, or knowledge is called _____.
    (a). Page 228. Factual.

    a. schema

    b. exemplar

    c. functional fixedness

    d. self-generated reference system

26. Brewer and Treyens (1981) showed subjects into an office for an interview. The office had no items such as books or computers but did have strange objects, such as a skull. Later, subjects were asked to recall the items that were in the office. The results showed that:
    (b). Page 228-229. Factual.

    a. subjects had an accurate memory of the strange objects but had noticed the absence of typical items as well

    b. subjects recalled seeing typical office items even when these typical items were not present but had poor memory for atypical items

    c. most subjects reported remembering the atypical items, such as a skull, but could not specifically report seeing any typical items but assumed they were there

    d. subjects had good memory for the conversation but very poor memory for reporting the contents of the office

27. Brewer and Treyens (1981) showed subjects into an office for an interview. The office had no items such as books or computers but did have strange objects, such as a skull. Later, subjects were asked to recall the items that were in the office. The above experiment demonstrates that people have:
    (c). Page 230. Factual.

    a. pragmatic inferences

    b. selective attention

    c. scene schemas

    d. integration processing

28. Schema theory is able to account for distortion in memory because of its assumption that:
    (b). Page 235. Factual.

    a. information from real experiences is never perceived accurately because it is a function of attention

    b. schemas guide selection and interpretation of new information so that its encoding is consistent with one's schema

    c. repression is a defense mechanism proposed by schema theory

    d. we perceive sensory reality through the perspective of our schemas

29. The SP+T theory assumes that when given information, relevant information is linked to a _____, information that does not typically fit is given a _____, and finally, atypical information is _____.
    (b). Page 238. Factual.

    a. episodic memory, red flag, discarded

    b. schema, unique tag, tagged as atypical

    c. neuron, new schema network, recoded

    d. module, presupposition, reprocessed

30. In schema theory, the idea that information is encoded selectively in accordance with an existing schema is known as:
>   (d). Page 232. Factual.

    a. subjective perception

    b. repression

    c. Piagetian period

    d. selection

31. SP+T stands for:
>   (c). Page 237. Factual.

    a. storage processing which adds transformation

    b. spatial perception with time

    c. schema pointer plus tag

    d. selection, processing, and thematic intrusions

32. The four processes proposed by schema theories are:
>   (a). Page 235-236. Factual.

    a. selection, abstraction, interpretation, integration

    b. encoding, transformation, storage, retrieval

    c. encoding, integration, distortion, storage

    d. presuppositions, inferences, integration, gist

33. In the SP+T model, given the following story, you are most likely to remember:
>   (a). Page 238. Conceptual

>   "The couple was seated at a cozy table in the corner of the restaurant. The wine had been served, and they toasted each other. When the waiter arrived, he spilled tomato soup in the lady's lap. After fussing around, the meal resumed. They had Baked Alaska for dessert, and they paid the check and left."

    a. for immediate recall, you will remember the spilled soup; later, you will recall the typical events

    b. all of the details immediately and later only the gist of the story

    c. that the couple did not tip the waiter

    d. that the couple was young, engaged, had Baked Alaska, and that she wore a white dress

34. In the SP+T model, given the following story, the SP+T model would predict that the reader is most likely to remember the atypical events at immediate recall, and later, the more typical events will be recalled. The reason for these predictions is that:
    (c). Page 238. Conceptual

    "The couple was seated at a cozy table in the corner of the restaurant. The wine had been served, and they toasted each other. When the waiter arrived, he spilled tomato soup in the lady's lap. After fussing around, the meal resumed. They had Baked Alaska for dessert, and they paid the check and left."

    a. baked Alaska, tomato soup, and white dress are all visually imageable and encoded with the event

    b. the pointer in the schema has pointed to the Hollywood schema version and tagged that version for memory

    c. the atypical action event is tagged in the schema and over time becomes less accessible as retrieval becomes dependent on the schema

    d. most people's restaurant schemas include vivid details of real-life events

35. Which of the following is NOT an assumption of schema theory?
    (b). Page 235. Factual.

    a. prior knowledge is activated and used when a new event or information is encountered

    b. since events are usually universal, people have the same or very similar schemas, which results in information being encoded the same for different people

    c. memory is not passive but is altered by reconstructive processes which occur at retrieval

    d. schemas are units which develop from experiences over time and can change with new experiences

128

TRUE-FALSE

1. With both presuppositions and inferences more is remembered than was actually said.

    (true).

2. Advertisements are cleverly constructed to promote faulty inferences.

    (true).

3. Temporally ordered schemas are called time-action sequences.

    (false).

4. It is possible to alter your memory of an accident by merely phrasing the questions in such a way that it forces you to make presuppositions which are not true.

    (true).

5. A restaurant schema could consists of your knowledge of entering, waiting to be seated, ordering, eating, paying, tipping, and leaving.

    (true).

6. You are more likely to remember atypical items in a room than you are typical items that you would think belong in the room.

    (false).

7. If I gave you a story to read and then gave you an immediate recall test, you most likely would remember the details of the story.

    (false).

8. After the development of schemas, the neural networks are determined in a concrete fashion; thus, new schema can develop, but old ones cannot be changed.

    (false).

9. A response bias is where you are likely to biased to respond a particular way depending on what the researcher wants you to do, or how a question is phrased.

    (true).

10. If you are given a story titled "Helen Keller," you are likely to remember details concerning visual and hearing impairment that were not in the original story.

    (true).

11. The advertisement that you "can't buy a stronger pain reliever than Anacin," implies that Anacin is the best pain reliever available.

    (true).

12. If the lawyer says to the witness, "Did you see the gun?" versus "Did you see a gun?" it causes people who heard the first sentence to presuppose that a gun was present at the scene.

    (true).

13. Elizabeth Loftus demonstrated that eyewitness testimony for events is usually very accurate regardless of the phrasing of the test questions.

(false).

14. It is clear that misleading information can change what a witness reports.

(true).

15. A spatially organized schema contains knowledge concerning how things are organized in space.

(true).

ESSAY

1. Bransford and Franks gave subjects sentences such as, "Three turtles rested on a floating log, and a fish swam beneath it." Later, the subjects were given a sentence recognition test in which the new sentences stated what the old sentences had logically implied such as, "Three turtles rested on a floating log, and a fish swam beneath them." Subjects recognized the new sentences as old. They concluded that logical inferences had been encoded with the original event. Can this finding be explained in the context of schema memory instead?

2. When Elizabeth Loftus showed subjects a scene of a car accident and asked them to estimate how fast the cars were going when they "smashed" into one another versus "hit," they reported higher speeds than the "hit" condition. At a later recall test, subjects in the "smashed" group report seeing glass at the accident even though there was not any. Loftus argues that a change in the memory representation occurred whereby the original event and the implied event are integrated into a new memory. How would you explain these results in terms of schema theory and its predictions?

3. Since schema theory predicts that all incoming information is interpreted in the context of existing schemas, it implies that memory can never be verbatim. What are the assumptions of schema theory that would address this issue?

4. What are the differences and similarities of encoding, processing, comprehending, and recalling a passage of written prose versus a verbal conversation?

5. You are reading an article about a lawn mower that rides on air but still cuts the grass in a typical way. The mowers are electric blue because the molecules from the air and ground interact only with this color chemical to make the machine float. It still has a rotating blade, and you have to walk behind it. The handles on it look more like bicycle handlebars, and in fact, it only has two large wheels with spokes in them. According to the SP+T theory, specifically how is this information encoded, what are the steps that would occur in processing this information, and what would be remembered about this mower.

CHAPTER 9
LANGUAGE

A. KEY WORDS

phonemes
design features
duality of patterning
displacement
speech acts
propositional content
thematic structure
phonology
syntax
semantics
morpheme
lexical content
grammar
phrase structure
noun phrase
surface structure

deep structure
transformational rules
pragmatic
constituent plans
articulatory program
phonemic restoration
echoic
telegraphic speech
linguistic competence
phonemic restoration
linguistic relativity
Whorfian hypothesis
traditional transmission
Broca's aphasia
Wernicke's aphasia

B. DEMONSTRATION/STUDENT ACTIVITIES

1. PHONEMIC RESTORATION

It is not difficult to demonstrate phonemic restoration to students. All that is needed is a tape player and a tape recorder. On the tape recorder, tape a 3 minute segment of the story in Handout 9-1. Once this is complete, put a second tape into the tape recorder and the original taped segment into the tape player. Start the tape player and record the taped segment again. However, read silently along with the recording, and as it comes to an underlined passage in the story, cough over the words, or crinkle a piece of paper near the tape recorder.

Play the cough-over tape to the students with the instructions that this is a tape that you recorded live at a seminar recently. Tell them that you apologize for the quality of the tape but that it is the content of the message you want them to be concerned about. When the passage is through, either read the passage or play the original taped segment, and ask students to write down which word in each sentence was obscured. They will not be able to tell you.

2. LANGUAGE ACQUISITION AND CONTEXT

This experiment is similar to an experiment in chapter 8 concerning how children acquire words given verbal contextual clues. Handout 9-2 has a list of clues that classify real words, only a nonsensical word has been used in its place. How many clues does it take before students guess the word?

HANDOUT 9-1

PHONETIC RESTORATION

RELAXATION AND FUN

A nice thing to do on a pretty summer's day is pack up some sand<u>wiches</u> and go on a picnic. It is great if you have company, but even if you must go a<u>lone</u>, it is a very therapeutic activity to do. First, choose a place where the scenery is nice even if it is in the center of <u>town</u>. There usually is always a park around some<u>where</u>. Sometimes even a graveyard is nice; it is at least always quite.

Some people go all out and have a fancy picnic bas<u>ket</u> with forks and knives and real plates. This is a won<u>derful</u> thing to do and makes you feel very special. However, a picnic is still a magical thing to do even if you just have a brown paper <u>bag</u>. It is however, nice to pamper your<u>self</u> if you can, so make sure the lunch is special. This does not mean that it has to be fattening with cho<u>colate</u> desserts and all. Even a salad can be made special. In fact, if you are on a diet, a pic<u>nic</u> can be just the thing to make that impoverished lunch seem kingly.

While you eat, think about all the beauty around you and try not to be agi<u>tated</u>. If things at work or home are bothering you, give yourself permiss<u>ion</u> to not think about them for the next hour. Problems sometimes can be solved much easier if you get a fresh new ap<u>pro</u>ach. So, for the time that you have given yourself for lunch break, give your<u>self</u> a problem break also.

Eat slowly and savor the flavors. Con<u>cen</u>trate on what it taste like, and do not gobble it down without a thought. Make the food, the scenery, and the whole experience a pampering event. Do not forget during the whole process to appreci<u>ate</u> yourself also. Think about something that you like about yourself and compliment yourself on it. Relax, have fun!

HANDOUT 9-2

WORD ACQUISITION

WORD 1

1. Most everybody has a rishid.

2. Sometimes very little children are too little for real rishids.

3. Rishids come in all different sizes and styles.

4. There are rishids for men and a different one for women.

5. If you have a rishid on the street, you have to be very careful.

6. If you have a rishid, you can see many different sights.

7. It is very healthy to be on a rishid for a long ride.

8. The hardest thing about a rishid is going up a hill.

9. Some people even enter rishid races and go for miles.

10. Most people like to ride a 10-speed rishid.

WORD 2

1. Leckets come in all sizes and shapes, but they are all still small.

2. It is easy to lose your leckets.

3. Most people have lots of leckets.

4. I have office leckets and house leckets.

5. Women usually keep their leckets in their purse.

6. If a lecket breaks off in a lecket hole, you have to call somebody to fix it.

7. If you lock your leckets in the car, it is usually a lot of trouble.

8. You can have a lecket ring and carry all your leckets with you.

9. Sometimes you can peek through the lecket whole and spy on people in the next room.

10. I have a front-door lecket and a back-door lecket.

C. ADDITIONAL RESOURCES

1. Suggested Readings

Fromkin, V., & Rodman, R. (1983). *An introduction to language* . New York: Holt, Rinehart and Winston.

Vygotsky, L. S. (1960). *The development of higher mental processes.* Moscow: Academy of Pedagogical Sciences, RSFSR.

Vygotsky, L. S. (1978). *Mind in society.* Cambridge: Harvard University Press.

2. Videotapes

Language. From *The mind series*, PPS Film Services, 1320 Braddock Place, Alexandria, VA, 22134.

The mind of man, Part 4, British Broadcasting System, c/o Films Incorporated, 773 Green Bay Road, Wilmette, IL, 60091.

Language. Films for the Humanities and Sciences.

3. CD-ROM

Normal communication acquisition: An animated database of behaviors. New York: Insight Media.

D. CHAPTER 9 TEST ITEMS

MULTIPLE-CHOICE

1. _____ is the name for a design feature of language which allows us to refer to events in the past or future.
   (b). Page 243. Factual.

   a. Repression

   b. Displacement

   c. Phonemic restoration

   d. Projection

2. Three elements of human communication which operate in a speaker-listener communication include all of the following EXCEPT:
   (c). Page 243. Factual.

   a. speech acts

   b. proposition content

   c. logical relativity

   d. thematic structure

3. A sentence can serve several functions. It can request for information, convey intentions, command, make assertions, make verbal commitments, etc. These functions refer to:
   (a). Page 243-244. Factual.

   a. speech acts

   b. grammar

   c. syntax

   d. semantics

4. The particular information conveyed by a sentence is called the _____ of that sentence.
   (b). Page 244-245. Factual.

   a. informational context

   b. propositional content

   c. thematic structure

   d. distinctive feature

5. Which of the following statements concerning Hockett's design features of language is NOT true of the language abilities of nonhuman primates.
    (c). Page 261. Factual.

    a. they are able to produce language which has a reflective quality

    b. they are able to meet the productivity requirement

    c. they have shown traditional transmission

    d. none of the above, they are able to perform all of the above

6. The smallest distinctive sound unit of language is a:
    (d). Page 246. Factual.

    a. prototype

    b. pheromone

    c. morpheme

    d. phoneme

7. The pauses typically observed in human speech serve to:
    (d). Page 249. Factual.

    a. indicate the distinctive features of morphemes

    b. mark different bases

    c. transform the surface structure into deep structure

    d. indicate something about the phrase structure of the message

8. The smallest speech units that carry meaning are called:
    (b). Page 246. Factual.

    a. phonemes

    b. morphemes

    c. prototypes

    d. concepts

9. In the simple word CATS there are 4 phonemes and _____ morpheme(s).
    (a). Page 246. Conceptual.

    a. one

    b. two

    c. three

    d. four

10. A sentence consist of two basic phrases called:
       (b). Page 249. Factual.

   a. a first phrase and a second phrase

   b. a noun phrase and a verb phrase

   c. a noun phrase and an adjective phrase

   d. a verb phrase and an adverb phrase

11. If you use run-on sentences and improper tense, you will be violating the rules of:
       (d). Page 247. Factual.

   a. semantics

   b. phonics

   c. framing

   d. syntax

12. After several martinis in a trendy night club, David's new companion asks if he would like to drive her
    white Jaguar to her fancy beach condo to see her etchings. This situation best illustrates the importance
    of _____ in affecting the meaning of indirect speech acts.
       (d). Page 244. Conceptual.

   a. contiguity

   b. content

   c. contact

   d. context

13. The various vowel sounds that can be placed between a "p" and an "n" produce words such as *PAN,
    PEN, PIN, AND PUN*. These various vowel sounds represent different:
       (a). Page 246. Conceptual.

   a. phonemes

   b. syntactics

   c. morphemes

   d phrase structure of the message

14. The surface structure of a sentence may be linked to its deep structure by applying:
       (b). Page 250. Conceptual.

   a. phrase structure analysis

   b. transformational rules

   c. base string analysis

   d. syntactical rules

15. The fact that the sentence, "Rock music can be the pits," can be interpreted in more than one way illustrates the need for a distinction between:
   (c). Page 250. Conceptual.

   a. episodes and events

   b. schemas and gist

   c. surface structure and deep structure

   d. geology and music

16. According to Clark and Clark, speech is typically planned and executed in a five-step sequence. Which of the following is NOT one of the five steps?
   (d). Page 252. Factual.

   a. discourse plan

   b. sentence plan

   c. articulation

   d. instructional plan

17. An experimenter replaces certain single sounds in a meaningful sentence with a coughing sound. Subjects are later unable to tell where in the sentence the cough occurred, evidently having restored the "coughed over" sounds. This phenomenon is called _____ restoration.
   (b). Page 254. Factual.

   a. phrase

   b. phonemic

   c. thematic

   d. contextual

18. The spontaneous utterance of a variety of elementary speech sounds by infants is called:
   (b). Page 254. Factual.

   a. syntax

   b. babbling

   c. telegraphic speech

   d. phonetics

19. During the earliest stage of speech development, children:
   (d). Page 254. Factual.

   a. speak in single words that may be barely recognizable

   b. begin to imitate adult syntax

   c. make speech sounds only if their hearing is unimpaired

   d. must learn to associate particular sound symbols with   particular aspects of their environment

20. Between _____ months of age, normal infants can produce all the phonemes that make up a language.
    (c). Page 253. Factual.

    a. 1 and 4

    b. 2 and 6

    c. 6 and 9

    d. 9 and 12

21. Sara is 2-years-old and says things like "want milk," "ball here," and "doggie gone." These are examples of:
    (c). Page 255. Conceptual.

    a. babbling

    b. artificial syntax

    c. telegraphic speech

    d. phonetic speech

22. Once a child learns a word for something such as "ball," everything they see that is similar is called "ball." This is because they:
    (a). Page 256. Factual.

    a. overgeneralize language to other items with shared features

    b. imitate the incorrect speech patterns of others

    c. use certain grammatical rules in sentence construction

    d. receive inadequate reinforcement for correct language usage

23. When a child is able to produce all and only those sentences of a given language they are said to possess:
    (c). Page 256. Factual.

    a. telegraphic speech

    b. grammatical rules

    c. linguistic competence

    d. phonemic restoration

24. In order to combine words into grammatically correct sentences, one needs to adhere to proper rules of:
    (b). Page 256. Factual.

    a. semantics

    b. syntax

    c. framing

    d. phonetics

25. According to _____, the structure of one's language leads one to view and think about the world in particular ways.
    (c). Page 258. Factual.

    a. Chomsky's theory of structure

    b. psycholinguistic theory

    c. Whorfian hypothesis

    d. Vygotsky's cultural model

26. The fact that when we hear the sentence, "The little, old man who lives in a crooked house, is crooked," we can recognize two different meanings for the word *CROOKED* demonstrates the importance of:
    (b). 248-249. Conceptual.

    a. syntax

    b. semantics

    c. morphemes

    d. linguistic relativity

27. According to the Whorfian Hypothesis:
    (d). Page 258. Factual.

    a. language is determined in infancy and childhood

    b. thoughts shape our language

    c. linguistic proficiency influences our social status

    d. language shapes our thoughts

28. The pattern of language dysfunction in an Alzheimer's patient would tend to indicate that:
    (a). Page 266-267. Factual.

    a. there are various levels of language organization distinctive to a particular area of the brain

    b. they first have Wernicke's aphasia then Broca's aphasia

    c. the first have Broca's aphasia then Wernicke's aphasia

    d. they lose only their ability in naming objects

29. For most human adults, language functions are localized in the brain region of:
    (b). Page 264. Factual.

    a. linguistic cortex

    b. left hemisphere

    c. right hemisphere

    d. corpus callosum

30. A split brain usually results from:
    (b). Page 265. Factual.

    a. schizophrenia

    b. surgical severing the corpus callosum, which connects the two hemispheres

    c. Wernicke's aphasia

    d. depression

31. If a split brain patient is shown a picture of a hammer which is projected in the right hemisphere and a picture of a dog in the left hemisphere, he can:
    (a). Page 265. Conceptual.

    a. name the hammer and match the picture of the dog on a recognition test

    b. label the dog and the hammer

    c. label the dog and match the hammer of a recognition test

    d. not be able to recognize either, but retrieve a verbal label for both

32. Two diseases caused by damage to the left hemisphere of the brain are called:
    (b). Page 266. Factual.

    a. linguistic relativity

    b. aphasia

    c. linguistic incompetence

    d. syntactic structural displacement

33. A person with _____ aphasia can understand the semantic content of a sentence if it is semantically phrased, but they cannot produce a sentence that is grammatically correct.
    (d). Page 266. Factual.

    a. Wernicke's

    b. Whorfian

    c. Chomsky's

    d. Broca's

34. A person suffering from _____ aphasia can produce grammatically correct speech, but their semantic content is nonsensical.
    (a). Page 267. Factual.

    a. Wernicke's

    b. Whorfian

    c. Chomsky's

    d. Broca's

35. A patient and neurological psychologist had the following conversation:

Doctor: What do you do for a living?
Patient: I am a seriat.
Doctor: You mean a blacksmith?
Patient: Yes, a seriat
Doctor: And what do you do there?
Patient: I work on a feriat.
Doctor: You mean an anvil?
Patient: Yes, a feriat.

The doctor diagnosed the patient as having:
(c). Page 266. Conceptual.

a. neural linguistic deficit

b. Broca's aphasia

c. Wernicke's aphasia

d. Alzheimer's disease

TRUE FALSE

1. The fact that we can talk about the past or future in language is called displacement.

    (true).

2. Phonemes are composed of about 12 distinctive features.

    (true).

3. Adult humans can produce about 100 phonemes, but English language uses only about 45 out of the possible 100.

    (true).

4. Language is composed of three basic parts: phonology, syntax, and semantics.

    (true).

5. Words like *GOODNESS* consist of one morpheme.

    (false).

6. Analyzing a sentence into its various phrases is called semantics.

    (false).

7. The deep structure of a sentence describes the sequences of phrases in a sentence as it is actually spoken.

    (false).

8. When a sentence was heard with certain parts of key words replaced with a cough, subjects did not recognize at which place a cough occurred. This is called phonemic restoration.

    (true).

9. Two-word speech by young children is also called telegraphic speech.

    (true).

10. According to Benjamin Whorf, language determines thought.

    (true).

11. Research has shown that in some cases it is possible to teach a chimpanzee to speak like a human child.

    (false).

12. One chimpanzee named Washoe is able to form over 100 words in American Sign Language.

    (true).

13. Language and speech are usually lateralized in the right hemisphere.

    (false).

14. A Broca's aphasia patient can produce sentences that are syntactically correct but semantically unintelligible.

(false).

15. A Wernicke's patient produces sentences which are fluent phonetically and syntactically but not semantically.

(true).

ESSAY

1. When people use hand gestures during conversation, they can either use emphasis gestures called BEATS which illustrate the syntactic structure or phrase structure of the language, or they can use iconic gestures, which illustrate the semantic content of the message. It has been found that Broca's and Wernicke's patients' gestural communication suffers from the same dysfunction as their verbal production. Describe what the two patients would sound and look like while communicating information about their summer vacation.

2. Describe the findings on animal language, and discuss why or why not this is "real" language.

3. If language determines thought as proposed by Benjamin Whorf, does this mean that children do not think until they acquire language? Discuss this in terms of the strong and weak version of the Whorfian hypothesis.

4. Describe the process of language acquisition in children.

CHAPTER 10
REASONING AND PROBLEM SOLVING

A. KEY TERMS

counter-factual thinking
formal logic
functional fixedness
syllogistic reasoning
mental model
probability theory
representativeness heuristic
conjunction fallacy
productive thinking
insight learning
task environment
problem space
ACT
task environment
incubation

validity
deductive reasoning
inductive reasoning
conditional reasoning
convergent thinking
divergent thinking
availability heuristic
Gestalt
reproductive thinking
persistence of set
operator
production
analogical reasoning
problem space

B. DEMONSTRATION/STUDENT ACTIVITIES

1. INCUBATION EFFECTS IN PROBLEM SOLVING

This experiment demonstrates the effects of problem solving and incubation periods. Students will be given a problem which is found in Handout 10-1 and asked to work on it for either 15 minutes or 30 minutes. After the initial study-work period, they are to stop working and do something else for either a time period of 30 minutes or 3 hours. After this time, they are to return to the problem and work on the solution for as long as they wish.

There are four groups of students in this experiment. Assign an equal number of students to each of the four cells in the matrix found in Handout 10-1. Tell them to work on the problem initially for *ONLY* the time period they are assigned to. After an incubation period of either 30 minutes or 3 hours, according to their assigned group, they are to return to the problem and try to solve it. Generally, since this requires out of class time, students are not motivated to complete this project unless it is their own project or they are offered extra credit for participation.

Discuss this experiment in the context of strategies used during the initial problem solving and after incubation. Were students consciously aware of processing during the incubation period?

2. TRANSFER OF KNOWLEDGE IN PROBLEM SOLVING

Handout 10-2 has a matchstick problem which can be solved without clues. However, it can be solved faster if students can use prior knowledge and transfer this to the problem solution. Divide the class into three groups, and give them the following sets of questions. Ask them to rate each question as to the truth or falseness of each statement. After completion of the questions, give them the handout, and time the groups as to how long it takes to solve the matchstick problem. This can be discussed in the context of fact-oriented and problem-oriented problem solving as discussed in the text.

SET 1

1. A tulip only blooms in the winter.

2. A match can be used to burn paper.

3. Mathematics includes the study of algebra.

4. A house only has 4 sides.

5. There are 4 quarters in a whole.

SET 2

1. A square has 4 individual sides.

2. Each side of a square is of equal length.

3. Two cojoined squares would have 7 sides.

4. Each angle of a square is 90 degrees.

5. Four squares would be made up of 16 sides.

6. Five squares would be made up of 16 sides.

SET 3

1. Sixteen matches can make 4 squares, if every square has 4 individual sides.

2. Two cojoined squares can have 7 sides, if they share one side.

3. Two squares should have 8 sides, if none of their sides touch.

4. Five squares would be made up of 16 sides, if two of the squares share two sides.

5. Five square can be made into 4 squares, if all the squares have 4 individual sides.

INCUBATION EFFECTS IN PROBLEM SOLVING

The following seven letters represent an infinite, sequential pattern. What are the next two letters?

O T T F F S S ? ?

Assign students to one of the following four cells. Scoring consists of (1) whether or not they solved the problem and (2) how much time it took them to do so.

Solution: The next two letters are *E* and *N* which stand for eight and nine.

STUDY-WORK TIME		
	15 MIN	**30 MIN**
INCUBATION TIME **30 MIN**		
3 HOURS		

THE MATCHSTICK PROBLEM

The following matches are arranged so that they form five equal squares. The task is to make the five equal squares into four equal squares. You have to move two matches and the two matches must be used in the new squares. Which two do you move?

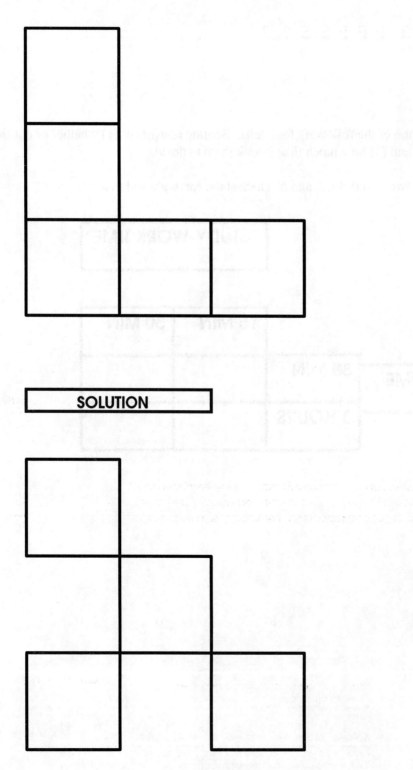

SOLUTION

C. ADDITIONAL RESOURCES

1. Suggested Reading:

Birch, H. G., & Rabinowitz, H. S. (1951). The negative effect of previous experience on productive thinking. *Journal of Experimental Psychology, 41,* 121-25.

Mayer, R. E. (1992). *Thinking, problem solving, cognition.* New York: W.F. Freeman & Company: New York.

Sternberg, R. J. (1985). *Human abilities: An information processing approach.* New York: Freeman & Company.

Sternberg, R. J. (1988). *The triarchic mind: A new theory of human intelligence.* New York: Viking Press.

2. Videotapes

Intelligence: A complex concept. CRM, McGraw Hill Films, 110 Fifteenth Street, Del Mar, CA, 92014. *Further approaches to learning.* Films for the Humanities and Sciences.

CHAPTER 10 TEST ITEMS

MULTIPLE-CHOICE

1. One example of problem solving which would discount the normative model would be:
   (c). Page. 273. Conceptual.

   a. reproductive thinking

   b. logical reasoning

   c. insight learning

   d. persistence of set

2. The primary difference between a normative model and descriptive models of reasoning is:
   (a). Page 273. Factual.

   a. a rule system versus nonrational thinking such as beliefs, attitudes

   b. deductive versus inductive thinking

   c. abstract thought versus concrete thinking

   d. all of the above are differences

3. If asked " are there more deaths per year due to murders or due to cancer of the digestive system", more people would answer murders. This erroneous answer would be due to:
   (b). Page 283. Conceptual.

   a. probability bias

   b. the availability heuristic

   c. conditional probability

   d. a mental set

4. A decision based on a representative heuristic could be compared to a decision based on a/an:
   (d). Page 283-284. Conceptual.

   a. inductive reasoning process

   b. schema

   c. mental set

   d. both b and c could be correct

5. Tom is an outdoor person with a great love for nature. He likes to hike, campout, fish, swim, and look for wildflowers. If you were to guess what Tom's occupation, you might be more likely to choose forest ranger over business executive. This decision would be based on:
 (a). Page 283. Conceptual.

   a. representativeness heuristic

   b. prototype theory

   c. availability heuristic

   d. probability theory

6. A reasoning problem which contains IF THEN statements is known as reasoning:
 (d). Page 275. Factual

   a. syllogistic

   b. deductive

   c. inductive

   d. conditional

7. The inability to solve a problem because you can only see the practical purpose of an object and not all of its possibilities is called:
 (c). Page 288. Factual.

   a. availability heuristic

   b. probability theory

   c. functional fixedness

   d. schema set

8. For Gestalt psychologists, problem solving consisted of:
 (d). Page 292. Factual.

   a. rejecting productive thinking and engaging in reproductive thinking

   b. rejecting reproductive thinking and engaging in productive thinking

   c. using availability heuristic to reason toward probability thinking

   d. transfer of inductive knowledge to all problem solving

9. Regardless of how the problem is represented, the key to a successful solution lies in how the problem is:
 (c). Page 290. Factual.

   a. generated or selected

   b. constrained or restricted

   c. represented or interpreted

   d. instigated or incubated

10. Problem space refers to:
      (d). Page 290. Factual.

a. a subject's mental representation of the problem

b. the various solutions that may be attempted to solve a problem

c. the various ideas or hypotheses that a person might develop about a problem

d. all of the above

11. In looking for transfer of problem solving solutions, the best performance results from problem-oriented:
      (b). Page 295. Conceptual.

a. information processing

b. priming

c. mental set

d. reasoning

12. A/an _____ refers to a sequence of operators that takes the problem solver from the initial state of problem solving to the goal state.
      (d). Page 290. Factual.

a. production

b. reproduction

c. mental operation

d. operator

13. The formal rules of logic are most applicable to:
      (c). Page 284. Factual.

a. mental models

b. inductive reasoning

c. deductive reasoning

d. explain the availability heuristic

14. The production system of problem solving differs from the Gestalt approach to problem solving primarily in that:
      (a). Page 298. Factual.

a. prior experience is a necessary component

b. prior experience is not a necessary component

c. logic is not involved

d. insight learning is very important

15. John Anderson's theory, ACT, proposes that problem solving is a function of learning a cognitive skill. This skill involves:
     (a). Page 290. Factual

     a. turning declarative knowledge into procedural knowledge

     b. turning procedural knowledge into declarative knowledge

     c. converting reasoning skills into knowledge skills

     d. integrating reasoning, thinking, and procedures into one skill

16. Proceduralization of knowledge makes problem solving more efficient by:
     (c). Page 291. Factual.

     a. converting all thinking processes into one skill

     b. eliminating too many alternate answers to one problem

     c. reducing the conscious capacity demands.

     d. all of the above

17. A person's mental representation of a problem is called:
     (c). Page 290. Factual.

     a. response bias

     b. cognitive outlay

     c. problem space

     d. mental set

18. You are given a difficult problem to solve concerning production in a plant. You remember that when playing with your 4-year-old son last night you erected a bridge of Legos to carry more trucks from one side to the other and you realize that this is basically the same problem with the same solution, then you are using:
     (b). Page 293. Conceptual.

     a. incubation

     b. analogical thinking

     c. functional fixedness

     d. heuristic strategies

19. Archimedes was given a problem of determining whether the King's crown was pure gold or not. He could not think of any solution, so he went to take a bath. As he sank into the tub and his weight displace the height of the water, he realized that he could solve the problem. He had:
    (a). Page 295-296. Conceptual.

    a. an insight

    b. a conscious reorganization

    c. production thinking

    d. all of the above

20. If you have a brain teaser problem and cannot solve it, you might give up and go for a walk. While on this stroll, the solution suddenly appears in your mind. This is called:
    (b). Page 295-296. Conceptual.

    a. transfer of problem space

    b. insight

    c. hypermnesia

    d. conscious processing

21. Once you have learned a strategy for problem solving, you may continue to use that strategy even when it is not appropriate. This tendency is known as:
    (d). Page 289. Factual.

    a. heuristic

    b. incubation

    c. problem space

    d. persistence of set

22. Which of the following is most clearly an obstacle to effective problem solving?
    (c). Page 288. Factual.

    a. trial and error

    b. the use of heuristic

    c. fixation

    d. the development of prototypes

23. If you are given a box of matches, five thumbtacks, and a small birthday candle and your task is to mount the candle upright on a bulletin board without burning the board, you are not likely to think of the correct solution due to:
   (b). Page 288. Factual.

   a. faulty reasoning

   b. functional fixedness

   c. lack of deductive reasoning

   d. analogical mapping

24. The difference between functional fixation and persistence of set is:
   (d). Page 288-289. Conceptual.

   a. that fixation is a subconscious mental process that is automatic and hard to overcome

   b. resistance to change in mental processing is consistent with persistence of set, but not fixation

   c. persistence of set is a type of dyslexia whereas fixation is just maladaptive

   d. fixation refers only to the function of objects, while persistence of set can apply to any situation

25. If you are given a set of common objects and a task to solve with these objects, and if you can use these familiar objects in a novel way, then you do not have:
   (a). Page 288. Conceptual.

   a. functional fixedness

   b. logical mislocation

   c. strategy deficit

   d. a low IQ

26. When children are taught that a good way to remember something is to rehearse it, they apply this strategy to all new learning, even when making other processes may be more effective, such as imagery or semantic associations. This insistence on maintaining an ineffective method of problem solving is known as:
   (a). Page 289. Conceptual.

   a. persistence of set

   b. detour resistance

   c. functional fixedness

   d. infantile amnesia

27. In solving the following problem, "Yellow is to lemon as _____ is to avocado," a subject is involved in going from a base to a target domain. This is known as:
    (a). Page 293. Conceptual.

    a. analogical mapping

    b. transfer of learning

    c. persistence of set

    d. task environment

28. Which of the following is NOT considered a good suggestion for problem solving?
    (c). Page 296. Factual

    a. remembering the problem

    b. understanding the problem

    c. using frustration as a pushing tool

    d. identifying alternative hypotheses

29. Gestalt psychologists have placed a bunch of bananas out of the reach of a caged chimpanzee. All they have supplied the chimp with are two sticks which fit together as a rake. When the chimp cannot initially retrieve the food, it pouts, whimpers, and gives up. Suddenly, the chimp jumps up, fits the two sticks together, and obtains the food. This is known as:
    (b). Page 295-296. Conceptual.

    a. analogical mapping

    b. insight learning

    c. fruit schema

    d. Sapiens reaction

30. _____ is the description of the problem as presented to the subject.
    (d). Page 290. Factual.

    a. Perceptual set

    b. Insight presentation

    c. Problem space

    d. Task environment

31. The two types of reasoning used in problem solving are:
    (b). Page 274. Factual.

    a. logical; hypothetical

    b. deductive; inductive

    c. atmosphere effect; verbal attack

    d. spatial; temporal

32. Sherlock Holmes would use all the general clues to focus on one suspect. This is the same as going from the general to the particular. Sherlock used:
    (a). Page 275. Conceptual.

    a. deductive reasoning

    b. inductive reasoning

    c. persistence of set

    d. mental models

33. Functional fixedness, according to Gestalt psychologists, would be a special case of:
    (b). Page 286. Conceptual.

    a. mental model

    b. reproductive thinking

    c. productive thinking

    d. information processing

34. Which of the following is NOT a general characteristic of problem solving from the information processing perspective?
    (c). Page 289-290. Factual.

    a. aspects of the task environment

    b. mental representation of the problem as a problem space

    c. transfer of prior information to the problem set

    d. selection of an appropriate operator.

35. If you are trying to get your pupil to transfer a solution from one set of problems to a similar set of problems, they are probably going to do better if you:
    (a). Page 295. Conceptual.

    a. give them a prior set of problems which set up a condition-action, or problem-oriented set

    b. give them a prior set of fact-oriented problems

    c. give them an unrelated set of problems

    d. give them a prior set of related problems but in another format, such as mathematical

TRUE-FALSE

1. You are more likely to make a decision based on representativeness heuristic rather than probability theory

   (true).

2. The validity of an inductive conclusion is probabilistic whereas the validity of a deductive conclusion is certain.

   (true).

3. An anagram, such as *TARIL,* is a type of problem where all the elements must be reordered in order to solve it. This is called an analogical mapping.

   (false).

4. Normative models of reasoning are rule-based theories of reasoning.

   (true).

5. Heuristic processes, such as representativeness, are examples of normative models of reasoning.

   (false).

6. Changing the way a problem is portrayed can aid problem solving. This is known as problem representation.

   (true).

7. A mental representation of the problem and its solutions is known by the information-processing approach as a problem space.

   (true).

8. Human beings are always logical and are not prone to make errors on reasoning tasks.

   (false).

9. Master chess players are able to reconstruct a chess pattern from memory much better than a novice player.

   (true).

10. Transfer of problem solutions from one set of problems to another is typical in most situations.

    (false).

11. Gestalt psychologists emphasize the importance of insight in problem solving.

    (true).

12. The description of a problem as presented to the subject is called the problem space.

    (false).

13. The task environment is the amount of time that a subject is allowed to solve the problem.

    (false).

14. The Gestalt psychologists proposes that reproduction thinking is the most creative type of problem-solving behavior.

    (false).

15. A sequence of events which takes a person from an initial state to the goal state in problem solving is known as a production system.

    (false).

ESSAY

1. Expert performance entails a different style of problem solving than that of the novice. Describe these differences, and describe which are the more efficient processes and why.

2. Explain the difference between normative and descriptive models of problem solving.

3. Subjects in an experiment by Gick and Holyoak were given a problem concerning destroying a tumor using radiation which most were unable to solve. However, another group of subjects were given a story prior to the problem which had similar elements in the story to the problem solution. What did this do to the performance of these subjects, and what is the explanation for the results?

4. Ellis has identified five rules concerning problem solving. What are these rules, and how are they to be applied to a problems like the Buddhist monk problem?

5. Sometimes when a person has successfully solved a problem, there is a tendency to repeat the solution in new situations. This is known as persistence of set. Explain the phenomena of persistence of set and determine the differences in this and functional fixedness.

CHAPTER 11
COGNITION, EMOTION, AND MEMORY

A. KEY WORDS

mood congruent effects   dysphoric
selective reminding   mood-state-dependent effects
network theory   schema theory
resource allocation theory   contingency judgments
mood induction   eyewitness testimony
flashbulb memories   arousal

B. DEMONSTRATIONS/STUDENT ACTIVITIES

1. INDUCTION OF EMOTIONAL STATES

There is physiological data that shows that enacting certain facial responses that are appropriate to an emotion can create that emotion in the subject. The entire class can participate in this experiment. Divide the class in half and assign one group to be the experimental group. The experimental group will all have to have an extra pencil or pen. Ask the experimental group to take the pen, and when you start the experiment, bite the pencil with their teeth as far back in the mouth as is comfortable.

You should collect in advance 24 photographs or drawings from magazines or books, etc. There should be eight pictures that depict happy, joyful, fun, or comical scenes, eight pictures with a sad, depressing, or frightening topic; and eight neutral pictures. You may use color and black and white shots, but if you use black and white, make sure that each category has an equal number.

Instruct the students that you will be showing them some pictures and that they are to rate the pictures on a scale of 1 to 10, with 1 being very low and 10 being very high, on how pleasant they find the pictures. Ask the experimental group to place their pens in their mouths and start the pictures. Allow about 5 seconds between each picture.

At the end of the experiment, calculate the scores given to each of the three categories by both groups. The pencil group will have rated the happy and neutral pictures as being more pleasant than the control group. Discuss this in the context of network and schema theory.

2. REACTION TIME AND EMOTIONAL CONTENT IN WORD ASSOCIATION TASK

In this experiment, you will demonstrate that words with high emotional content take longer to respond to than normal words without emotional affiliation. Ask for one to two volunteers to do a word association test. Send the volunteers out of the room while you explain to the class what the reaction to emotionally laden words is likely to be. Subjects will either have increased reaction time to the emotional words, they may repeat one of the words already mentioned, either a list word or one of their response words; or not be able to think of a word at all.

You may assign a student to time how long it takes the volunteer to produce a word association for each of the words and another student to mark if one of the other two responses occur.

If you use two volunteers, ask one student to wait where they cannot hear the first student being tested. Instruct the student that you will give them a list of words, and they are to say the first word that comes into their mind as quickly as possible. The words are found in Handout 11-1.

REACTION TIME RESPONSES AND EMOTIONALLY LADEN WORDS

COFFEE
CHAIR
SALT
CRICKET
FRUIT
*TORTURE
ENVELOPE
PICNIC
*RAPE
PILLOW
*MURDER
LOCOMOTIVE
*THIGH
ONION
HAIRNET
*SEX
ZEBRA
BATHTUB
*BREAST
BICYCLE
*ABORTION
LIGHT
*SPERM
HOUSE
COMPUTER
RADIO
*CONDOM
CHILD
CAMERA
*GENITALS
MARKET
BLANKET
*PELVIS
CARPET
INFINITE
*INCEST
CHICKEN

C. ADDITIONAL RESOURCES

1. Suggested Readings

Houston, J. P., (1986). *Fundamental of learning and memory* (3rd ed.). New York: Harcourt Brace Javanovich.

Kleinsmith L. J., & Kaplan, S. (1963). The interaction of arousal and recall interval in nonsense syllable paired-associate learning. *Journal of Experimental Psychology, 65,* 124-26.

Winograd, E. & Killinger, W. A. (1983). Relating age at encoding in early childhood to adult recall: Development of flashbulb memories. *Journal of Experimental Psychology, 112,* 413-22.

Zajonc, R. B. (1980). Feelings and thinking. *American Psychologist, 35,* 151-75.

Zajonc, R. B. (1984). On the primacy of affect. *American Psychologist, 39,* 117-23.

2. Videotapes

Neuropsychology. Films for the Humanities and Sciences.
Critical thinking and emotions. New York: Insight Media.

D. CHAPTER 11 TEST ITEMS

MULTIPLE-CHOICE

1. Research on emotional influences in memory and cognition has increased since 1975 because:
        (d). Page 303. Factual.

   a. the area is recognized as important

   b. methodological approaches have developed

   c. there is a need to explain how emotion influences memory

   d. all of the above

2. Which of the following theories best explains mood congruent effects where you remember details of one or the other characters in a story?
        (b). Page 320. Factual.

   a. network theory

   b. schema theory

   c. resource allocation

   d. propositional theory

3. _____ refers to the fact that a happy person is more likely to remember happy rather than sad material.
        (d). Page 305. Factual.

   a. Mood contingency

   b. Mood-state dependency

   c. Mood retrieval

   d. Mood congruence

4. Joy Bliss read a story about one happy and one sad character. Joy believes that the happy character is the central figure in the story and that the story contains more statements about the happy character. Joy's reactions illustrate _____ effects.
        (a). Page 305. Factual.

   a. mood-identification

   b. mood-fluctuation

   c. mood-reversal

   d. mood-sublimation

5. Joy Bliss read a story about one happy and one sad character. Joy is in a particularly happy mood that day. Joy believes that the happy character is the central figure in the story and that the story contains more statements about the happy character. On the next day, while in a neutral state, she will probably recall _____ facts about the sad character in the story.
　　　(b). Page 305. Factual.

　　a. more

　　b. fewer

　　c. the same number of

　　d. no

6. Bower hypnotized subjects into either a happy or sad mood and read them a story about two college men, one happy and one sad. Later, when they had returned to a neutral mood, they were asked to recall the story. What he found was:
　　　(c). Page 305. Factual.

　　a. the happy men remembered both characters equally well, while the sad subjects only remembered the sad character

　　b. the sad subjects remembered both characters equally well, while the happy subject remembered only the happy character

　　c. both subjects remembered details about the character that was congruent with their hypnotized state

　　d. both subjects showed very poor memory due to the state of hypnosis

7. Bower explained the mood-congruent findings by:
　　　(a). Page 305. Factual.

　　a. selective reminding

　　b. mood enhancement

　　c. schema theory

　　d. state dependency

8. The Bower, Gilligan, and Monteiro study on mood congruence found that the effect was the greatest when the subjects were in:
　　　(b). Page 305. Factual.

　　a. a happy mood

　　b. both a happy and sad mood

　　c. a sad mood

　　d. an angry mood

9. If you read a passage of a story about a happy character and a sad character and you are depressed, which character are you going to remember more about?
    (a). Page 305. Conceptual.
    a. the sad character

    b. the happy character

    c. there will be no difference in memory for each character

    d. she probably will not remember either character very well

10. Which of the following theories best explains mood-dependent effects on memory where there is better memory for material learned in one emotional state and tested in the same emotional state?
    (b). Page 320. Factual.

    a. association theory

    b. schema theory

    c. resource allocation

    d. propositional theory

11. Mood-state-dependent effects in memory are best seem as:
    (b). Page 306. Factual.

    a. strong

    b. fragile

    c. schematic

    d. organized

12. When subjects are given a drug which induces a particular mood, they found that subjects remembered more at the test session if they were in the same mood as they were when they studied the material. This is known as:
    (a). Page 306. Factual.

    a. mood-dependent effects

    b. hot cognitions

    c. conditional memory

    d. mood contingency

13. Roger will take a cognitive test at his school tomorrow. He is likely to score _____ if his emotional state during the test is _____.
       (e). Page 304. Conceptual.

   a. best; sad

   b. worst; happy

   c. best; happy

   d. mediocre; neutral

   e. best; neutral

14. When subjects were either in a happy, sad, or neutral mood over a five-trial memory test, Leight and Ellis (1981) found that:
       (c). Page 307. Factual.

   a. the neutral state performed the worst

   b. that the happy state performed the best

   c. that both happy and sad state performed worse than the neutral state

   d. all of the above

15. Studies on depressed mood states that vary in the effortfulness of the task show the greatest decrements in recall performance when the task is
       (b). Page 311. Factual.

   a. easy

   b. difficult

   c. intense

   d. problem solving

16. In an experiment on the effects of mood on memory for elaborative or basic verbal material, the results showed:
       (d). Page 311. Factual.

   a. memory for basic material is the same for the sad and the neutral subjects at a short (7-second) encoding period

   b. memory for the elaborative material is better for the neutral subjects at both short (7-second) and long (10-second) encoding periods

   c. memory for basic material increases for neutral subjects at longer encoding times

   d. all of the above

17. In material that requires both high effort and low effort to encode, researchers found:
    (c). Page 311-312. Factual.

    a. that sad subjects could do as well on both types of material

    b. that neutral subjects did just as well on high-effort material as low-effort material

    c. that sad subjects remembered the high-effort material no better than the low-effort material

    d. effort is not a factor in memory and emotions

18. The primary conclusion from the above experiments is:
    (a). Page 312. Factual.

    a. that sad emotional states require too much capacity of energy to allow normal memory effects

    b. that subjects in a happy state of mind can encode and retrieve material better than those in a neutral state

    c. that the tasks involved in the tests were too confounded to draw definite conclusions.

    d. all of the above

19. Which of the following theories could best explain the effects of organization and mood where depressed people do not organize material for memory?
    (c). Page 316-317. Factual.

    a. network theory

    b. schema theory

    c. re-resource allocation

    d. propositional theory

20. Which of the following theories best illustrates why when you experience a bad mood you might recall the time you ran a stoplight because you were in a bad mood?
    (a). Page 320. Conceptual.

    a. network theory

    b. schema theory

    c. resource allocation

    d. propositional theory

21. Alloy and Abramson show that depressed subjects, when making judgments of contingency, are _____ neutral mood subjects.
  (c). Page 324. Factual.

  a. less accurate than

  b. as equally accurate as

  c. more accurate than

  d. none of the above

22. The exposure to emotionally laden words in a word list is likely to result in:
  (b). Conceptual, based on the demonstration in Handout 11-2.

  a. the inability to perceive these words when they are presented subliminally

  b. a difference in reaction time in a word association test to these words from nonemotional words

  c. change in a person's memory for certain words according to the emotional state at the time of study

  d. all of the above

23. Easterbrook's theory of memory and emotion which predicts that as emotional arousal increases there is a progressive restriction in the range of cues to which a person attends is called:
  (b). Page 327. Factual.

  a. emotional attentional deficit

  b. cue-utilization

  c. network restriction

  d. mood arousal effect

24. The cue-utilization theory predicts:
  (d). Page 327. Factual.

  a. moderate levels of arousal can improve memory

  b. in moderate emotional arousal, relevant cues will be attended to while irrelevant cues will not

  c. higher levels of arousal results in fewer cues being utilized

  d. all of the above

25. The recall of vivid, very important, emotionally arousing events is called:
   (a). Page 327. Factual.

   a. flashbulb memory

   b. infantile amnesia

   c. mood-arousal effect

   d. retrieval nostalgia

26. If you can recall where you were when you heard that the space shuttle *Challenger* had exploded, this memory is called:
   (b). Page 327. Conceptual.

   a. retrieval aftershock

   b. flashbulb memory

   c. network relay

   d. affective recall effect

27. Pillemer points out that flashbulb memories:
   (d). Page 327. Factual.

   a. help to communicate the sense of being present at an event

   b. add face validity to the testimony

   c. evoke a more sympathetic response

   d. all of the above

28. Depression is related to anxiety in that:
   (b). Page 329. Factual.

   a. anxiety creates depression

   b. depressed people are frequently anxious

   c. anxiety and depression make people's cognitions self-focused

   d. all of the above

29. It has been found that anxiety affects performance by:
   (c). Page 329. Factual.

   a. increasing arousal so that on high-level tasks, people perform better

   b. increasing capacity for performance

   c. producing performance decrements especially in high-demand tasks

   d. decreasing memory performance on word lists recall

30. When normal, depressed, and anxious people are asked to estimate the likelihood that some unpleasant event would happen to themselves or to other people, the results showed:
    (a). Page 329. Factual.

    a. depressed and anxious people thought the unpleasant events would happen to them but not to others

    b. depressed people thought that the unpleasant events would happen to the normal people first

    c. the depressed people were accurate in predicting that unpleasant events happen to everybody

    d. the anxious people only thought that all unpleasant events occurred to them

31. When people are anxious, it is found that their anxiety levels _____ their learning.
    (d). Page 330. Factual.

    a. facilitated

    b. debilitated

    c. depending on the nature of the task, could both interfere with or facilitate,

    d. had no effect on

32. Eysenck reported that anxiety both harmed and helped learning performance because anxiety:
    (a). Page 329-330. Factual .

    a. increases distracting thought and increases arousal levels, which lead to more allocation of effort to the task

    b. caused an increase in a neurotransmitter serotonin which has ambiguous results on performance

    c. reduced the energy people had but that motivation played a role in performance

    d. all of the above

33. In Eysenck's two-process idea of anxiety and performance, the two processes include:
    (b). Page 330. Factual.

    a. memory and thinking

    b. distraction and arousal

    c. fear and joy

    d. realism and pessimism

34. Arad performed an experience where subjects had to classify items in a high and low stress condition. The results showed that:
    (c). Page 330. Factual.

    a. low-stress subjects pay less attention

    b. high-stress subjects attend only to relevant features

    c. high-stress subjects pay less attention to distinctive features but also overgeneralize

    d. all of the above

35. If retrieval of information is dependent on the mood, it has been argued that the mood and the information have to be encoded at the time of learning. This is most consistent with the theory of:
   (d). Page 308. Factual.

   a. contingency response

   b. attentional deficit

   c. feature set

   d. encoding specificity

TRUE -FALSE

1. There is strong evidence that indicates that flashbulb memories are always good both immediately after the event and again after a long time period.

   (false).

2. People who are depressed are more realistic in their perception of events than are nondepressed people.

   (true).

3. Generally, anxiety creates arousal, which leads to increased performance in high-demand tasks.

   (false).

4. Subjects reading a story about a happy and sad character usually recall the happy character regardless of the reader's mood.

   (false).

5. It can take you longer to respond to an emotionally laden word in a word association test than a nonemotionally laden word.

   (true/ based on demonstration 2).

6. If you study for a test when you have been given some mood-altering drugs, you will recall more of that material if you are in the same drug-altered mood at the time of testing.

   (true).

7. People in a neutral state of mind will recall less than people in a sad state of mind on a memory test.

   (false).

8. If you are in a happy mood, you will rate pictures as being more pleasant than people in a neutral mood.

   (true, based on demonstration 1).

9. One reason that depressed people do worse on memory for sentences that are elaborative is that they have less cognitive resources than normal.

   (true).

10. It has been shown that depressed people recall less than neutral people on a recall test purely due to an encoding effect.

    (false).

11. The schema theory of emotion states that depressed people recall less than normal people because they have limited resources available to use.

    (false).

12. When depressed people are required to pay focused attention to a task, they do even poorer than usual.

    (false).

13. A flashbulb memory is a photographic memory of some emotional episode in a person's life.

    (false).

14. According to the cue-utilization theory, depressed people are more restricted to the range of cues available to cue memory than are nondepressed people.

(true).

15. Strong levels of emotion are likely to impair memory, especially if the task is more difficult.

(true).

ESSAY

1. In an experiment, subjects read a story which included both a happy and sad character. Bower found that the recall of the characters was greater for the one who was congruent with the reader's mood. Explain this finding, and discuss it in terms of network and schema theory.

2. Discuss the similarities and differences in the three theories of memory and cognition.

3. When depressed people do worse than nondepressed people on a recall test, does this effect result from emotional effects on encoding, retrieval, or both?

4. Do the emotional states of anxiety produce different effects on memory than those found to occur from depression? Why or why not and what is the evidence that demonstrates your position?

5. How would each of the three theories of emotion and cognition explain flashbulb memory effects?